Reflections of Ourselves

American University Studies

Series XXVII
Feminist Studies

Vol. 1

PETER LANG
New York • Bern • Frankfurt am Main • Paris

Sharon Howell

Reflections of Ourselves

The Mass Media
and the Women's Movement,
1963 to the Present

PETER LANG
New York • Bern • Frankfurt am Main • Paris

Library of Congress Cataloging-in-Publication Data

Howell, Sharon
    Reflections of ourselves : the mass media and the
women's movement, 1963 to the present / Sharon Howell.
      p. cm. — (American university studies. Series
XXVII, Feminist studies ; vol. 1)
    Bibliography: p.
  1. Women in mass media — United States. 2. Feminism
— United States. I. Title. II. Series.
P94.5.W652U65   1990   305.4'2'0973 — dc19   88-12696
ISBN 0-8204-0523-X   CIP
ISSN 1042-5985

CIP-Titelaufnahme der Deutschen Bibliothek

Howell, Sharon:
Relfections of ourselves : the mass media and
the women's movement 1963 to the present /
Sharon Howell. — New York; Bern; Frankfurt
am Main; Paris: Lang, 1990.
  (American University Studies: Ser. 27,
  Feminist Studies; Vol. 1)
  ISBN 0-8204-0523-X

NE: American University Studies / 27

Printed by Weihert-Druck GmbH, Darmstadt, West Germany

to Betty and John Howell . . .

and to the memory of Ruth and Willard Kauth, whose vision touched the lives of so many women.

Table of Contents

Chapter

Chapter

Chapter

Acknowledgments

Like all books, this one has grown out of my involvement with many people and ideas from many places. But by more than anything else over the last ten years, my thinking has been shaped by the women and men with whom I have worked for political and social change. The National Organization for an American Revolution has been central in my thinking about social movements. From it I have gained a tremendous appreciation for the capacity of human beings to continue to advance and question our world. The lives and works of James and Grace Boggs, Freddy Drake Paine, and Patricia Coleman-Burns have encouraged me to look beyond superficial understandings. Listen to Women for a Change and the Reweaving the Web study group have enabled me to be more open to the spiritual struggles of women than I ever could have been without their patience and energy. In a less organized fashion, my thinking has been challenged by the images put forward by artists in women's music. I am especially grateful to Nancy Vogl for her probing of ideas as well as her artistic vision.

I owe much of my decision to share these ideas with a wider audience to Janice Fialka who reminded me of the importance of looking critically at all we have accomplished over these last twenty years.

My overall perspective on the development of movements through stages and the importance of metaphor is the direct result of countless conversations and discussions with Bernard Brock, who shared in the creation of this work.

Carolyn Forbes and Pauline Redmond and Jack Miller of the Anvil Press have contributed in countless ways to my thinking and their labors made this work possible.

Preface

The women's movement happened in the everyday lives of people. The changes and challenges it brought were reported, analyzed, probed and interpreted by commentators across the country. The very act of reporting the movement helped shape the meaning it was to have for all of us.

This study looks at how the women's movement was seen through the eyes of the mass media. The images the media created provided an essential coherence to the emerging identity of women that evolved over the last two decades.

CHAPTER I
A Rhetorical Movement

The women's movement has been called everything from an oxymoron to a communist plot.[1] It is said to be the result of undersexed neurotics or oversexed fanatics. It is cited as the reason why families are falling apart and as the basis of new, more solid family values. It has been pronounced dead on several occasions. It has been derided and denied, often by women themselves, in the most untraditional of female roles participating in the most untraditional of female activities, politics. And its impact has been felt by hundreds of thousands of ordinary women and men who have been forced to reexamine basic aspects of their lives by the simple declaimer, "I'm not a women's libber, but..."

For more than two decades the women's movement has defied easy definition. Yet is has infused the major political movements of our time with important philosophical, strategic and tactical questions. It is a source of tremendous intellectual creativity stimulating such traditional disciplines as history, literature, philosophy and sociology. Artistic and cultural endeavors have been challenged with new and exciting perspectives. The movement has motivated women and men to act and think differently about themselves, their responsibility to society and their relationships to other human beings.[2]

Yet by 1982 virtually everything the women's movement struggled for had been turned around. The ERA, which seemed inevitable in the early 1970s died a slow, inglorious death, buried under images of women warriors and potty jokes. Day care centers were closing across the country. Rape crisis centers and domestic violence shelters no longer garnered community support. Popular songs proclaimed the virtues of domestic life. Anti-ERA, anti-abortion, pro-family, and fundamentalist religions all stressed women's "proper place" and gained adherents every day. And the movement itself had become increasingly white, middle-class, professional and bewildered by its own inability to respond to the "moral majority." The women's movement, which burst forth in the 1960s and matured in the 1970s with an energy that rocked some of the fundamental areas of our lives, had by the 1980s become impotent and isolated.

The progressive thrust of the movement has been blunted. Its basic ideas and programs are not only being rejected, they are openly attacked. Unlike any other social movement in the last two decades, the women's movement and all it represents have become the target of the "new right." As a result, the emergence, development and subsequent attack on the movement reflect one of the most profound shifts in American political life in this half of the 20th century. It mirrors the rise and fall of American Liberalism. Consequently the women's movement reveals some of the deepest currents in our social and cultural life as a nation and provides a glimpse into the contours of the struggles emerging in the coming decade. It is for this reason that we should analyze the contemporary women's movement for it reflects the development and death of the liberal philosophy which has governed America for over 50 years.

Beginning in the heart of the civil rights movement and spanning two decades of social, political and economic turmoil, the women's movement has addressed such basic issues as work, family, sex, race and class. It has confronted or avoided each of these in a multitude of ways. In the process, no matter how successfully or unsuccessfully, how cogent or chaotic, the movement has become inextricably woven into the history and development of American life in this century.

Rhetorical Dimensions

The importance of the movement in understanding American life is matched by its elusive nature. Extending over a generation, chronicled and discussed in literally hundreds of books, articles, pamphlets and magazines, embracing divergent and often contradictory ideologies, carrying on its life in hundreds of thousands of mimeographed documents and countless conversations, it is an awesome subject. Yet its very vastness and diversity lend to the importance of rhetorical analysis. For within all the chaos and confusion, particular rhetorical dimensions of the movement emerge. Like the civil rights movement which gave it birth, the essential unity of the movement came from the simple fact that above all else the primary issue it faced was rhetorical in nature. The thrust of the movement has been the creation of a new female identity. The burning question underlying all of the activities of the last two decades has been an exploration of the issue: What does it mean to be a woman? The probing of this question, at first hesitantly, often painfully and sometimes angrily, has been the guiding force behind the growth and development of the movement.

And it is this search for a new female identity which has given the movement its rhetorical dimension. The problem confronting the movement was and is rhetorical. It required a perceptual change. This is outlined by Hope in her analogy with the black movement:

> Both the black movement and the women's move-
> ment arise from a perception of reality. Their op-
> pression is biologically based. Black oppression is
> based on race, the condition of blackness. Female
> oppression is based on sex, the condition of
> femaleness. Since the oppression finds its source
> in primarily conditions of biology—generally
> unalterable facts of identity, both movements have
> faced the issue in the only way possible, rhetorical-
> ly. Because no legislation nor any weapon can make
> black white and women men, both groups had to
> redefine an oppressive identity.[3]

Thus the driving force of the movement has been the development of strategic responses to ultimately transform the female identity into a positive, integrated conception that expresses some greater dimension of what it means to be a human being and female. Or quite plainly as Betty Friedan explained in her discussion of why she wrote the *Feminine Mystique,* society had reached a point where human beings had to ask, "What does it mean to be a man or a woman?" She describes the circumstances when she points to the necessity of confronting the question of identity:

> It happened at that moment in time from historical
> necessity; the evolution of society, the technology
> made by man had brought woman to this jumping
> off point: a massive crisis of identity brewing
> already in my mother's generation came to a head

in my generation of American Women.[4]

Women who had for centuries been clearly defined within the domestic, private sphere had through the 19th and 20th centuries found themselves increasingly freed from the necessities of the home. Technologies of all kinds in the home and in the work place converged to both eliminate many of the burdens which had kept women in the home and to remove many of the barriers which had kept them out of the workplace. The definition and identity which had been taken as natural for generations were suddenly called into question. If not wife, mother, daughter, temporary worker looking for a husband, keeper of domestic virtue and caretaker of home and hearth, what then was woman?[5]

This inward probing of identity was coupled with a serious challenge to basic institutions within society. The creation of a new female identity was never viewed solely as a perceptual change or an inner transformation. Rather, personal identity was clearly understood as the result of institutions and attitudes that circumscribed society and as tied to the restructuring of basic areas of public life. The movement intended to influence institutions, values and mores through direct political action. As a result, like all social movements, it had to address questions of attracting new members, devising policies and programs and adapting to new situations that its own activities helped to create. In the course of this activity fundamental concepts of political action, leadership, power and organization were all challenged in ways that reveal some of the greatest strengths and greatest weaknesses of the movement.

The women's movement thrust women into the world as a public actor and in so doing raised a challenge to the very nature of politics itself. This challenge initially emerged as much out of practical necessity as theoretical clarity. Faced with the mounting contradictions of being political-ly active and female within radical organizations during the height of the civil rights movement, women were compelled to question basic assumptions about politics. On the one hand women had begun to get a new sense of themselves as political actors. Organizing voter drives, participating in marches and sit-ins, often risking and in some cases losing their lives along with the men, and doing the countless day to day tasks from producing leaflets to mailing letters to being sure everyone had a place to sleep and eat, women in the early 1960s began to grasp political activity through the texture of their own participation. At the same time as this experience was enlarging their sense of themselves as political beings, women recognized that their contributions to the movement were being restricted and dominated by men. Women found themselves typing leaflets, not writing them, copying speeches not giving them, and making coffee and food for the men who did the "real" political analysis. In the course of this women began to sense a growing disparity between the ideals of their organizations and the realities of their own political lives. More and more they saw that the desire of men to exercise and maintain leadership was a way to shut women out. Based on this experience women initially challenged and then ultimately rejected male concepts of leadership. Women began to identify the conscious or unconscious strategies that men employed to quiet women and keep them in their place: the use of inattention or ridicule, the minimizing of remarks and ideas that women advanced as trivial, the patronizing or hostile response to those few women with the courage to express themselves. In opposition to this, the movement in the early formative period attempted to create a supportive, encouraging environment in which women would feel safe to contribute their thoughts and ideas. Stressing the importance of all women contributing, leadership and the exercise of control or direction were consciously eschewed. The spirit of this new concept of leadership was captured by Marge Piercy in her poem "Councils."

She begins:

> We must sit down
> and reason together
> We must sit down
> Men standing want to hold forth.
> They rain down upon faces lifted.
>
> We must sit down on the floor
> on the earth
> on stones and mats and blankets.
>
> There must be no front to the speaking
> no platform, no rostrum
> no stage or table
> We will not crane to see who is speaking
> perhaps we should start by speaking softly
> The women must learn to dare to speak.

In this way the movement tried to create an environment for women to speak without fear or hesitation. To do so they rejected the models of male leadership that became totally associated with dominance and ridicule. But as a result the movement also rejected and actively prohibited the rise of any individual women leaders as well. To be sure several women have emerged as spokespersons over the years: Betty Friedan, Gloria Steinem, Robin Morgan, Marge Piercy, Angela Davis, Kate Millet, Gerta Lerner and Judy Chicago to name only a few. Yet these women, representing diverse perspectives and areas of action, some with organizational affiliations and others not, do not constitute a leadership in the traditional (male) sense of the word. They represent diverse and contradictory ideologies and while they give public voice to concepts and strategies, they cannot initiate coordinated mass activity that would incorporate the totality of the movement. Nor could they agree upon any united program or direction for the movement.

The movement having provided a safe space for women to find their voices brought ideological and emotional pressure to bear to be sure no single voice would outshine the united chorus. Sara Evans, in her excellent discussion of the origins of the women's movement, describes the duality in these early efforts to create new concepts of leadership based upon new principles of equality and supportiveness.

> Women who developed an ability for public leadership...received harsh criticism for being stars. On the one hand if they shared the movement's anti-authoritarianism, they quickly withdrew, stung by the criticism. Naomi Weisstein, for instance, felt that the movement had given her a voice and then taken it away again; as a result, the women's revolt wasted the very talent it needed most. And on the other hand, women who refused to withdraw from public view operated as spokeswomen...when in fact there was no structural means of holding them responsible for what they said and did.[7]

Because of the ideological commitment to avoid leadership and domination of one another the movement created one of its most serious contradictions: a new style of leadership became confused with no leadership. Spokespersons, not leaders, became the public voices of the movement and these individuals became more and more isolated from any larger political base.

Along with the absence of leadership, the supportive environment created within the movement fostered an unwillingness to criticize or challenge the ideas of other women. The goal was to get women to speak. What they said, why they said it, what it meant to the development of the movement was often considered irrelevant. Thus while developing clearly identifiable and divergent political ideologies, women created a context of support. They never seriously criticized one another or the basis for the ideas they were advancing. This lack of self criticism and unwillingness to challenge one another further compounded the subjective basis of the movement and allowed for the creation of all kinds of ideas, often the result of unclear, unchallenged and uncritical thinking. And the movement as a whole, despite its defeats in the last few years has remained remarkably uncritical of its own subjective nature. With the exception of Elshtain and her critique of the sloppy untruths which have provided the basis for much of feminist theory, a serious critique of the evidence and reasoning for the theoretical underpinnings of contemporary feminist thought—of all persuasions—has been avoided within the confines of the movement itself.[8]

Despite the absence of leadership and the refusal to engage in any rigorous intellectual criticism and debate, the attack on male concepts of leadership contained within it one of the most important philosophical contributions of the women's movement. Experiencing in their daily lives the tremendous disparity between beliefs and actions, women openly rejected the notion that human beings could separate their political life from their personal life. "The personal is political" became a rallying cry which shattered the neat male separations between political and private life. Men could no longer avoid housework, childcare or the travesty of their own relationships by claiming they had to be involved in more important political work. The charge of hypocrisy became a potent weapon in reshaping the basic assumptions about what constituted the political realm and the practice of "correct" political behavior. Yet even the power of this concept was not without its negative implications. Having shattered the traditional boundary between the personal and the political, the movement developed in such a way as to become dangerously close to eliminating this division all together. However, the resurgence of intellectual and practical exploration of what constitutes political action became a major contribution of the movement to political thought.

The conscious avoidance of leadership, the emphasis on creating a supportive environment and the exploration of personal lives and feelings as the basis for political action combined to further stress the rhetorical dimensions of the movement. Strategies of action rather than personalities or proposals became central. Consciousness-raising groups became the hallmark of the movement. Consciousness-raising replaced policy advocacy. This was not only the stylistic response to the ideology of the movement, but it was a practical necessity in developing and attracting membership. For while the initial phase of any movement begins with the recognition of solidarity and a collective common oppression, the particular role and place of women in American society meant that they had no shared rhetorical traditions, no commonly developed public spaces, no perceptions of themselves as an oppressed group with a common fate. Catherine Stimpson articulated this problem in the early stages of the movement when she commented:

> We must do much more arduous work to persuade women to recognize the realities of their lives. Few blacks still need consciousness raising. Our job is harder because white, middle-class women have had so many privileges and because the national impetus toward suburbia makes each home embracing its homemaker, not just a castle, but a miniature ghetto. Blacks have long celebrated their culture. We must discover if women have a commonly felt, supportive culture.[9]

Within the span of a very few years these isolated and middle class women, and thousands of others, responded with an outpouring of activity. Consciousness-raising groups sprang up all across the country. Sometimes beginning with a traditional coffee clatch and becoming formalized meetings, sometimes starting with a few friends who had come across the thousands of mimeographed guidelines for discussion distributed by budding women's organizations, or sometimes the determined result of politically active women forming caucuses, these groups became the heart of the early movement. As a result, no particular policy or set of policies, nor even a constitutional amendment, embrace the totality of the movement and its search for a new identity for women. The very nature of the movement and its aim require that policy considerations be viewed as secondary.

Thus the contours of the movement emerge not in the struggle for a particular bill nor even the Equal Rights Amendment. They come out of the many voices given force by manifestos, public letters and statements issued within the radical and new left communities, the countless demonstrations from Women's Equality Strike to Take Back the Night and the multitude of articles, books, pamphlets and quiet conversations that have become the expression of a new consciousness among men and women. In a very real sense, it is the talk of the movement that embodies its heart and direction.

Thus the contemporary women's movement is a particularly rhetorical movement. Its goal is to create a perceptual change—a new female identity. Its essence is expressed through its strategies and actions rather than it leaders and policies. Its membership is diverse and sometimes unwilling. It embraces a variety of ideological and political perspectives out of which it struggles to forge some unified central direction. It is these characteristics which make the contemporary women's movement particularly well suited for rhetorical analysis.

Major Divisions in the Movement

Out of the cacophony of positions the movement appears as diverse and uncoordinated. It embraces a variety of ideological and political perspectives. However, there is an underlying unity and coherence. While women differ on their perceptions of how social change should occur, the nature of women and the relationship between women and the larger society, all essentially are striving to develop a new, positive identity. Thus three general groupings merge within the broader movement. Each of these groups contains within it several different political tendencies, but the broad parameters outlined within each group give a sense of their general thrust.

The first group is the female radicals. These women come largely from within radical organizations, be they "old" or "new" left, and their primary emphasis is the creation of social change through revolutionary struggles. They see the role of women as only part of a larger struggle to transform the whole society. Essentially they adhere to the Marxist dictim (or some variation of it) that the success of a revolution is judged by how the status of women has been changed. It is to these female radicals that we owe the initial recognition of the oppression of women within not only the political world but within the larger society. Because of their political experience they were able to provide a conceptual vocabulary to identify and discuss relationships of power and exploitation.

Expanding and building upon many of the concepts and definitions from the female radicals, there emerges the second distinct grouping within the movement, the radical feminists. Like their counterparts, the female radicals, these women are committed to fundamental change within the social, political and economic structures of society. But they argue that any fundamental change must begin with a transformation of the status of women. For them, patriarchy is the major contradiction facing society. Their ideology, while sometimes basing itself on terms and concepts of the political left, is basically an attempt to develop a theoretical understanding of society and virtually all history from the perspective of the sexual division of labor. While this tendency represents a numerical minority within the movement much of the creative theoretical work (for better and worse) has come from them.

The largest and most visible of the women's groups is the liberal feminists. Unlike the other two groups, they do not advocate revolutionary change. They are essentially reformist groups. Even though they often use the term "revolution," they accept many of the basic assumptions of the society and focus their efforts on changing political institutions from within the "system." Most typically the membership of this group is characterized as white, middle-class and professional. They are concerned with establishing social, political and economic equality with men. They do not question the basic assumptions of how men have defined these spheres of human activity. The most visible organization within this branch is the National Organization for Women (N.O.W.). It is with this general group that most women, unaffiliated yet sympathetic, would identify.[10]

These rhetorical dimensions pose special challenges for criticism. For, like the movement itself, the traditional (and even less traditional) notions of rhetorical criticism do not bend easily to embrace the totality of the women's movement. It is a movement with no official voice, containing divergent and contradictory ideas and tactics. It expresses itself through a few major public acts or public policy debates. It is expressed most directly in talk and in literally hundreds of thousands of small publications, poems, plays, letters and articles. Fundamentally it is a movement which has been struggling to change not only social and cultural mores and values but to completely redefine what it means to be a woman.

14

NOTES

1. Karlyn Kohrs Campbell, "The Rhetoric of Women's Liberation: An Oxymoron," *Quarterly Journal of Speech* 59(February 1973), p. 74-86.

2. Edward B. Fiske, "Women's Studies Now Challenge Scholars' Long Held Beliefs," *New York Times,* 25 November 1981, p. 10.

3. Diane Schaich Hope, "Redefinition of Self: A Comparison of the Rhetoric of the Women's Liberation Movement and Black Liberation Movements," *Today's Speech* (Winter 1975), pp. 20-21.

4. Betty Friedan, *It Changed My Life* (New York: Dell Publishing Company, Inc. 1977), p. 23.

5. Sheila M. Rothman, *Woman's Proper Place: A History of Changing Ideals and Practices, 1870 to the Present* (New York: Basic Books, Inc., 1978), pp. 177-257.

6. Marge Piercy, "Councils," *To Be of Use* (Garden City: Doubleday & Company, 1969), p. 33.

7. Sara Evans, *Personal Politics* (New York: Vintage, 1980), p. 233.

8. Jeane Bethke Elshtain, *Public Man, Private Woman* (Princeton, New Jersey: Princeton University Press, 1981), pp. 256-57.

9. Hope, p. 19.

10. These categories have been drawn from Judith Hole and Ellen Levin, *Rebirth of Feminism,* (New York, Quadrangle, 1981) with the addition of the term liberal feminism. This group, so named by Elshtain, reflects the philosophic tradition of liberalism as well as claims an historic identity with early feminist struggles. Thus the term is more accurately descriptive.

CHAPTER II
On Rhetorical Method

The purpose of this study is to trace the evolution of the female identity through an analysis of the dominant metaphors emerging in the course of the contemporary women's movement. Consequently, there are three distinct fields of study that form the background for this inquiry: studies of social change and social movements; analysis of language and the use of metaphor; and historical evaluation and documentation of the movement. This chapter will examine all three areas to provide a context for the particular focus on the contemporary women's movement developed here. It will also discuss the specific methodology employed to document the metaphorical constructs as they emerged within the public media to give shape and direction to the movement.

Social Change and Social Movements

United action by large numbers of ordinary citizens to influence or change the direction of their society is a relatively recent phenomenon in human history. It was not until the beginning of the Eighteenth Century that such massive, purposeful activity became a part of the historical forces shaping the development of public life. The Eighteenth Century inaugurated an age of revolutions. Beginning with the American and then the French revolutions, theories of politics, economics and society have had to account for the reality of change brought about by the dramatic, often forceful actions of the masses of people.

While human history is filled with examples of changes in governments and societies, the uniqueness of revolution as a purposeful, united restructuring of the social order is clearly a product of the modern world. The uniqueness of this concept can be seen in the evolution of the word itself. The French Revolution gave the term its specific political meaning. Prior to that time, revolution was a word used to describe the actions of physical bodies in motion as in the revolution of the planets and stars. But the drama of people overturning the existing government and sources of authority made revolution a central fact of political life. It represents not only change, but a new beginning, with new forces able to exercise power in the political world. Hannah Arendt in her incisive discussion of the development of revolution summarized this political action:

> It was only in the course of the eighteenth-century revolutions that men began to be aware that a new beginning could be a political phenomenon, that it could be the result of what men had done and what they could consciously set out to do. From then on, a 'new continent' and a 'new man' rising from it were no longer needed to instill hope for a new order

of things. The *novus ordo saeclorum* was no longer a blessing given by the 'grand scheme and design in Providence,' and the novelty was no longer the proud and at the same time frightening possession of the few...it became the beginning of a new story, started—though unwittingly—by acting men, to be enacted further, to be augmented and spun out by their posterity.[1]

The reality of the storming of the Bastille, and later of the overthrowing of the Russian Czar and of the long marches through the Chinese countryside have infused the modern consciousness with vivid images of revolution and social change. As a result, the issue of revolution and change brought about by those who have historically been excluded from the public realm has become a concern of virtually every discipline studying the activities of human society.

The new actors brought onto the stage by revolution express themselves in countless ways. Individuals excluded from the exercise of public political power come together not only for the total restructuring of society but to achieve more limited or specific goals. The history of our own nation is filled with this kind of political and social action: the Great Awakening, the Abolitionist Movement, the Sufferage Movement and the Populists. Recently in this century we have seen movements by laborers in the 1930s, the civil rights and black power struggles of the 1950s and 1960s and the anti-war and women's movements of the 1960s and 1970s.[2] Each of these movements, responding to specific contradictions within the society, challenged fundamental concepts about the nature of human relationships and human activities. They were movements by "outsiders." They were movements by those who had no effective political voice in the established order. And they were movements in opposition to the direction, institutions or assumptions of the larger society.

It is out of efforts to describe, interpret and evaluate these human experiences that the systematic study of social movements began. Consequently, the theoretical assumptions behind any analysis of revolution or social movements with more limited goals are intrinsically related to perceptions of social change and the development of society. Basic judgments about the relationship between the individual and society, about the nature of change itself and about the human being as either an active or passive being underline divergent theoretical approaches. These assumptions cut across the neat dividing lines of the major disciplines that consider social movements: history, political science, sociology, psychology and social-psychology.

The philosophical perspective underlying this study is that of dialectical materialism/dialectical humanism. This philosophy, first articulated in *Racism and the Class Struggle* and later in *Revolution and Evolution in the Twentieth Century* is based on a particular understanding of social change. [3] It rests on the belief that social reality is constantly changing. This change comes about because of the emergence of contradictions growing out of human interaction with objective reality. It is out of conflicting ideas and methods for addressing these contradictions that individuals must choose one course of action over another. As a result human beings are constantly engaged in the process of arguing, persuading and cajoling one another. This is the essence of politics and of rhetoric. Conflict over ideas, policies, values and direction is essential for social growth. Inherent in this philosophy is the recognition that human beings live not only in a material world but in a socially constructed world expressing our unique capacity to symbolize our environment, to endow it with meaning and to make judgments and to reflect upon and evaluate our actions.

This philosophical outlook led me to rhetorical criticism. While it has only been in the last thirty years that rhetorical criticism has focused on social movements as a distinct phenomenon, it has added a particular depth and texture to the understanding of the process whereby people define their world and make judgments about how to act in it. Beginning with Griffin's now classic studies, rhetorical criticism focuses on the symbolic or rhetorical dimensions of movements. It offers a method to not only understand what social movements are, but how and why they function.[4]

Some Areas of Agreement

Virtually all disciplines agree that social movements begin by a rejection of the existing order. Social movements are "breaks" or disruptions in the ordinary course of events. They are efforts to change what has come to be accepted as normal and natural. Consequently movements are seen to have actual beginning points. It is at this beginning point where the disquiet in society is defined. Thus Griffin's "naysayer" is important not only because of what he initiates, but because in the act of saying No! he defines the purpose of the movement and provides the basis for a collective identification by those in opposition to the existing order. To Marx's concept of emerging contradictions and class consciousness, rhetorical criticism adds the symbolic definition and articulation of that contradiction.

Closely related to this idea of a beginning point in a social movement is the notion that movements proceed through developmental phases. From inception to consummation or through legitimization or redemption, numerous theorists agree upon the concept of stages of development. Binder, Griffin, Toch, Smelser, Gusfield, and Larson, while disagreeing on particular terms, all agree on the evolutionary quality of movements.[5]

On a somewhat broader level we have the conceptualization of these stages within a dramatic perspective or within metaphorical constructs. Borman's "rhetorical vision" illustrates this as does Burke's "stages of order." Rhetorical criticism has especially concentrated on developing methods to examine symbols as they shift from stage to stage. Thus much of the substance of critical analysis grows out of efforts to document and describe these shifting frames.[6]

There is also widespread agreement that social movements are purposeful activities. Burke's distinction between motion and action becomes important here as it helps to set apart the rhetorical or symbolic perspective from a more deterministic viewpoint sometimes expressed within other disciplines.[7] Movements are seen as more than the product of external forces. They are created through human choice and decisions, expressed and conducted through symbols and talk as well as actions. Social movements are seen as efforts to change the existing society through the mobilization of mass activity directed at the power relationships, norms and essential direction of the established order. This activity is not only a rejection of the existing order, however. It also poses a new direction contained within the "rhetorical vision." Yet the "new order" is not conceived of totally in material terms. It evokes images of the "quest for salvation" as in Griffin or the establishment of a "perfect order" as in Burke or Blumer.[8]

Thus rhetorical studies add the sense of moral tensions and visions to unite actors and lend purpose to their actions. Salvation, victimization, redemption and moral constraints become part of human motivation for change. Rather than seeing these as mere images of the superstructure, rhetorical criticism entwines the symbolic world with the material base, illuminating it at its best, obscuring it at its worst.

Order Versus Conflict

Once we move beyond these broad areas of agreement, however, the differences among theorists are as much a product of their orientation toward social change as they are the product of the particular emphasis inherent in the various disciplines. In general, theorists are either oriented toward conflict or order perspectives.[9] For those operating within a conflict perspective, social movements are seen as a legitimate means of problem solving. They are positive actions that are the inevitable result of living in a world in constant change and flux. They are part of the evolution of society and are welcomed as essential for growth. Dialectically based, conflict theorists realize there is no "resting point" in human development. Today's solutions become tomorrow's problems. In contrast to this, those theorists operating within an order perspective see social movement as disruptions in the orderly processes of change. Movements are illegitimate and destructive deviations from the natural order.

Within these two overriding images of social change, individual actors are portrayed in very different ways. In the conflict perspective, objective developments are highlighted. Forces are identified which "compel" people to first define and then attempt to resolve contradictions. Marx, of course, is the essence of this approach. However, these forces are never seen as wholly of a material character, either by Marx or later theorists. Rather, human beings are viewed as acting on issues of social justice, morality and ideals as well.[10] Cathcart poses the importance of moral tensions in the creation of social movements.[11]

Within the order perspective, individuals who move toward the collective resolution of conflict are characterized as psychological misfits as in Hoffer.[12] Actions in the public world are viewed as the result of unresolved personal complexities. Feurer is one of the strongest advocates of this viewpoint from the field of psychology.[13] And Toch, from the perspective of the social psychologist, identifies feelings of "disaffiliation."[14] Even Cantril, who takes a somewhat more dialectical approach, sees individuals as being personally susceptible to the "cause" due to their own private experiences.[15] In essence, because the movement itself is seen as deviating from the normal processes of society, those who are involved in its creation became characterized as personally deviant.

Material and Symbolic Tension

Rhetorical studies pose a constant tension between the material world and the symbolic world. While this tension is never resolved, most studies emphasize that rhetoric arises out of some actual contradiction or constraint which human beings attempt to name or define. Smelser talks of the "structural conduciveness necessary for social movements." He argues that the fluidity of the times, as well as the composition of the people at that moment in relation to those times are preconditions for periods of social unrest.[16] Earlier, Sherif and Sherif[17] gave a similar image of this tension when they talked of the necessary role of "out of the ordinary conditions" that are expressed in the conflict of values and the breakdown of norms that have heretofore held the society together. Roberts and Kloss as well stress the realities of inequalities that arise from the conflict of class, racial or sexual struggles which are then given voice and definition within the movement. In a certain sense, the more recent studies in genre provide an implicit recognition of the necessity of viewing rhetoric or symbols as growing out of particular circumstances.[18]

Language and Interaction

A social movement requires not only the recognition of discontent by one or two individuals but the articulation of that discontent in order to initiate collective action. Central

to any social movement is the creation of a collective definition of the problem and the communication of that problem
to the larger society. Smelser focuses on the mobilization
of the participants for action and has given a view of the
relationship among the participants as have Sherif and
Sherif in their efforts to study the means by which participants communicate. Even Simon's emphasis on leadership within the movement grows out of an understanding
of the importance of describing the inner dynamic of direct-
ing the movement.[19]

It is within the development of a symbolic perspective
that explores the necessity of internal unity and the attracting of the attention and resources of the larger society that
we are able to see movements as more than acts of rejection or rebellion. Burke, Duncan, Berger and Luckmann and
most recent theorists have put forward the importance of
communication and the manipulation of symbols.[20]

Studies of social movements from the perspective of
rhetorical criticism have become marked by the investigation of the symbols, language and acts that pervade the
scene and become a part of it. These acts are conceptual-
ized in various ways. Griffin talks of "efforts to alter the
environment." Smelser of the "mobilization of participants."
Borman of the "rhetorical vision." However called, it is these
acts which form the substance of the movement. They define
the sources of discontent and provide the visions for the new
order.

In the course of these studies, the *how* of the movement
becomes central. Symbols and signs take on an enlarged
significance. The talk of the movement becomes as important as the actual policy or change advocated. Even silence
takes on a new meaning within the larger rhetorical context
created by a movement. Hewitt noted that "by treating the
social order as partly a product of talk about it, we open
the way to view that social order as multiple and not
singular."[21]

As a result, the interaction of the movement becomes as important as the action. Here rhetorical studies have made their most unique contribution. Sherif and Sherif stress that the talk of the movement becomes the method by which the demands for change are expressed and by which "gripes" are aired. The talk provides a platform that is not only an analysis of prevailing conditions but a formulation of actions and a charting of the kind of course people should take to resolve contradictions. Osborn emphasizes the importance of rhetorical strategies on this level to polarize the sides and to identify the enemy through the employment of archetypal metaphors.[22]

Thus rhetorical criticism has carved out a unique sphere within the study of social movements. It has contributed to an understanding of how the scene becomes defined, how contradictions are named and how strategies are evolved. It has expanded the understanding of human action to express the inherent tension between the material and the symbolic world and recognized that movements of masses of people come to life through the interaction among the members of the movement as well as through the efforts to persuade one another and the larger society of the justness of the cause. Human beings are seen as purposeful actors, defining, interpreting, acting in their world not only because of material necessity, but because of the meaning which they have supplied to their own activity and relationships.

The Importance of Metaphor

This study begins within this tradition of rhetorical criticism addressing the role of symbols and symbolic action. In particular, the framework drawn upon is that which explores the relationship between language and action. Some of the most important work in this area is the exploration of metaphor as it lends meaning, coherence and purpose to human actions. Rhetorical criticism has been developing a growing body of work drawing upon metaphor to illuminate larger themes and perceptions. Some of the more important of these studies include Black's "The Second Persona," and Kathleen Hall Jamieson's, the "Metaphoric Cluster in the Rhetoric of Pope Paul VI and Edmund G. Brown." In both of these studies, metaphors are used as analytical tools to reveal deep, almost hidden ideological assumptions. Jenson's review of the "family metaphor" explores the strategic responses implied by metaphoric concepts and definitions. The work of Osborn, central to all these studies, has been particularly insightful in providing the foundation for the role of metaphor in shaping thinking as well as providing an elegance to description.[23]

The emphasis of this study is to bring together the growing understanding of the explanatory and analytic powers of metaphor with an analysis of the dynamic development of social movements. Precisely because social movements represent new beginnings, new activity and new actors, they have to be explained and justified to the participants and the larger society in terms that are known. This is the essential function of metaphor, to give the "new" meaning in terms of the already "known."

The Use of Metaphor

The power of metaphors to grasp and express contradictory and ambiguous ideas and events has long been recognized. In addition, metaphor has been understood as a way of moving from the known to the unknown. From Aristotle's earliest inquiries into the nature of language through Kenneth Burke to contemporary anthropologists and sociologists, the capacity of metaphors to lend insight and to convey a dimly perceived reality has become more and more valued as a way to expand our understanding of meaning in the human world.

Within the field of rhetorical criticism, a critical analysis of metaphor has been a major focus of our understanding of how language functions. Metaphors emerge to entitle and enliven discourse. They provide a basis for viewing movements, not as particular policies or acts, but as a complex web of meanings, emotions and motives that are contained in the "rhetorical vision." They also provide a means to approach movements from a holistic, strategic focus.

Burke, who offers us the most insightful, if oft-times maddeningly obscure discussion of metaphor, stresses the ability of metaphors to subsume a variety of complex and often contradictory concepts. In one of his rare moments of succinctness he states:

> ...they are marvelous short-cuts. They are short-hand, like higher mathematics. They can define a complexity quickly and easily—and without them we could at best vaguely sense a particular complexity.[24]

This ability of metaphors to capture the totality of things is discussed by Sapir and Crocker in their development of the "social use" of metaphor to convey complex meaning within society. They provide the following characteristics of metaphors:

1. It expresses an abstract idea in a concrete form. It offers a justification for the ideas and appeals to emotions that are required to enlist sympathy from larger environments.
2. It conveys a perception of the whole.
3. It moves from the known to the unknown.
4. Its ambiguity allows it to attract wide, diverse groupings.
5. It provides a mode of simultaneous awareness of events, ideas and emotions.[25]

Finally through the work of Lakoff we have most recently come to see the importance of metaphor not only as it conveys meaning but as it also embodies strategies for actions.[26] Metaphors enable us to grasp, clarify and connect ideas in ways that provide insight into complex and changing reality.

An analysis of the dominant metaphors emerging within the life of the women's movement provides an understanding of the essential coherence and direction of an otherwise amorphous phenomena. Metaphors become the basis for defining the direction of the movement, for analyzing the grounds on which new members are attracted and for defining its enemies. Within the subtle ambiguities and relationships inherent in the metaphors a new female identity emerges.

Each metaphor comes out of the varied voices of the movement—focusing the movement, adapting to the larger context and laying the basis for the next stage. Each grows out of and responds to the limitations of the previous metaphor, never wholly disappearing yet shifting in emphasis. And each metaphor posits essential philosophic and political concepts which become the core of various political tendencies. Taken together these metaphors represent the developing female identity which has come in the 1980s to challenge our concepts of men, women and political activity.

The Women's Movement:
A Particular Challenge to Rhetorical Criticism

There is, then, a large body of criticism devoted to an understanding of movements, be they historical, social, revolutionary or reformist. While the definition and direction of these studies is still the subject of lively controversy, there is no question that rhetorical criticism has an important contribution to make to our understanding of human experience.[27]

In the concern for definition, method and theory, however, there is a peculiar lack of self-reflection in light of some of the most important insights being developed by feminist scholars of all political perspectives. While there is no shortage of articles and books exploring the rhetoric of feminism, there has been little serious exploration of how feminism itself challenges rhetorical criticism. The basic theoretical underpinnings of rhetorical criticism have remained remarkable above the fray.

Both for the growth of the critical discipline and for the ability to evaluate what the women's movement means to an enlarged understanding of the human being as a public actor, rhetorical criticism can no longer avoid glancing inward.

The basic tenets of rhetorical criticism have grown out of an investigation of political or public discourse. Theories are drawn from reflection on politics as it is practiced. Yet there has been little questioning of the very nature of this political activity and how it has shaped our inquiry. The lack of critical examination of the categories of public and private becomes critical in any analysis of the contemporary women's movement. It is precisely in the effort to reshape these distinctions that the movement most powerfully struggles with the issue of the female identity.

This lack of reflection on the basic content of the political world was recently discussed by S. Michael Halloran in his fine review of the work of Richard Sennett. He notes that in the four years since Sennett first published *The Fall of Public Man* there has been only one reference in the *Quarterly Journal of Speech*. The only major theorist and critic to have advanced a discussion of these concepts has been Lloyd Bitzer.[28]

The conceptual distinctions between the public and private worlds has shaped how we look at political activity, what we define as political and how we have come to look at social movements. Thus our concepts of public action have been formed by male oriented, taken-for-granted assumptions. Both the limitations and insights of this perception frame our knowledge of social movements.

The limitations of this model quickly surface in the literature of social movements. It is assumed that the leaders of the movement express its essence. And often the method of exercising leadership is distinctly male. On a superficial level this is seen in Leland Griffin's refreshing examination of criticism and historical movements. Here we find Griffin contending that the forceful male "naysayer" initiates movements.[29]

On a deeper level, rhetorical criticism grows out of a concept of political action as practiced by men in the world that they have defined as public. It is at the nexus of public and private that the women's movement most explicitly rejected male ideas of politics, leadership and power.

The breadth and diversity of the movement requires a critical method which is able to embrace ideological ambiguity. It requires a method that will enable us to synthesize diversity and to deal with a tremendous volume of rhetorical activities. Finally it requires a method which will capture the nuances inherent in the evolution of a complex concept of what it means to be a human being and a political actor played out in a realm of human activity that is not always clearly acknowledged as political.

On Method

A study of the women's movement, then, poses theoretical and practical questions. When did it start? What are the critical strategies? What constitutes a body of rhetorical discourse that reflects the movement? In many ways the answers to these questions will have to be somewhat arbitrary, although certainly not uninformed. The basic conceptual framework will be Griffin's concept of stages as they are expressed within the metaphor of the movement.

First, the time period to be studied will be 1961 to 1981. It was in 1961 that President Kennedy established the Commission on Women reflecting a growing concern for the role of women in American society. Beginning at this point, the women's movement unfolds in a series of dominant metaphors that develop over two decades and serve to weave the strands of a new female identity.

These metaphors are formulated within the radical community and then fan-out to become part of the larger society. They become the basis for strategic actions or symbolic acts. They are evoked to justify actions or decisions and they serve as a way to describe scenes, actors or acts. Thus the metaphors function in three realms: description, justification and strategic response. In the descriptive realm metaphors are employed to explain actions or actors based on a clearly cited comparison. This description not only delineates essential characteristics based on comparison but also contains within it a host of related concepts and ideas implying specific justifications or motives as well as allowable strategies. A metaphor emerges, provides a basis for unity and coherence and then fades, replaced by another. Each becomes the means by which the movement explains itself to itself and by which the movement is made intelligible to the larger society.

Source of Rhetoric

The selection of materials that document the movement is difficult. On the one hand there is a wealth of material: speeches, books, plays, articles, organizational documents, position papers and artistic productions. Yet no single publication or set of publications embrace the total movement. Likewise the very diversity of the political groupings creates problems of selection. Among radicals and radical feminists, publications come and go. Speeches and position papers are doomed to gather dust in piles of mimeographed papers within the confines of organizations that lived for a year or two. Nor are the liberal feminists easy to track. Even major NOW conferences were never recorded or carefully documented. Speeches, often powerful and provocative, rarely went beyond an immediate audience. Friedan, for instance, was famous for two-hour speeches given extemporaneously.

However, because of the particularly important role the women's movement as a whole has played in the development of issues and events over the last two decades, it has received consistent and often indepth coverage in major periodicals. The *New York Times* has offered ongoing articles in several areas. Four distinct types of coverage have developed over the years.

1. General news coverage. Individuals, actions, events and trends that relate to women are regularly discussed.
2. In-depth analysis. This analysis occurs within three specific areas. The *Magazine* section provides a vehicle for discussion of the movement and its various tendencies from the most radical to the most reactionary. The *editorial section* is occasionally forced to comment on the movement and the *section devoted specifically to women* not only reports on the condition of women and the movement but becomes an object of its activity.
3. Book reviews. In the late 1960s and early 1970s the explosion of books for and by women forced its way into the *Times.* This phenomenon became a source of special comments along with the books themselves.
4. Letters to the Editor. Both the ongoing news coverage and the special sections of the paper pro-

voked letters from women who identified themselves as part of the movement. In this way, many of the more radical or less "newsworthy" ideas found their way into coverage.

These areas of coverage represent not only efforts by the *Times* to chronicle events, but also illustrate the attempt by the *Times* and the movement itself to become understood by a larger audience. The *New York Times* then offers a vehicle for monitoring the unfolding concepts of women and the activities of the movement. It covers the full spectrum of actors, motives and events. By systematically following the items listed under the category of women as indexed by the *Times*, it is possible to trace the development of the movement and its varying tendencies both from the direct comments and ideas of women and from the perspective of the journalists who attempt to understand and explain it.

Along with the *Times*, two other publications will be systematically considered. The first is the set of papers and ideas that were fundamental to the early articulation of the movement. Robin Morgan in her anthology, *Sisterhood is Powerful*, is the best source of these. *Sisterhood is Powerful* became the official Bible of the movement, drawing attention to its major concerns and documenting its fundamental ideas.

Finally, beginning in 1972 there is the publication of *Ms.* magazine. Growing out of the energy and imagination of the movement and signalling a new level of independent consciousness, *Ms.* was published to speak directly to the women of the movement. Despite its generally professional and upper-middle class bias, it has continued to be a voice for the movement and to offer insights into the ideas and actions of all aspects of the political spectrum.

All three sources will combine to provide the basic body of discourse to be analyzed. The *Times* will be reviewed by categorizing and coding all articles that appear under the key word women. Both *Sisterhood* and *Ms.* will be catalogued based on the coding system developed from the analysis of the *Times* and the effort to capture the functions of the metaphors in developing the movement.

Specific Analysis

In order to prevent as much as possible the superimposition of my own vision of the movement on the data, I will use a vigorous system of content analysis. All articles appearing under the *New York Times Index* heading of women will be read and coded. Based upon an analysis of the first 10 years of coverage, as well as the function of metaphors, a system to classify data will be established. The following categories are suggested: subject, role, description, political action, justification and opposition. Under subject the actual topic of the articles will be recorded. Role identifies the social functions ascribed to women, such as mother, homemaker, doctor, secretary. Description categorizes the adjectives used to describe the subject or role. These descriptions tend to form distinctive clusters. Political action notes the specific public action advocated such as letter writing, protesting, or establishing this or that program. Justification reflects the rationale for action or the basis for legitimatizing arguments. Opposition traces actual comments or critical attacks against the movement. Also articles discussing the opposition as an organized force will be noted. These groupings began to form patterns within categories. Shifts in clusters are noted as they indicate a change in the elemental unity. For example, justification for actions in the early period of the movement, as well as descriptive adjectives for women leaders, almost totally drew upon metaphors from the black power and civil rights struggles. By the mid-1970s almost no adjectives of this character were employed.

Ms. will be similarly catalogued. However, two important distinctions are to be made here. Special attention will be paid to both the frequency and intensity with which subjects were addressed. Some subjects recur over and over again. Other subjects, while occurring less frequently, will be noted if they combine a cover story with a special indepth issue or discussion. Thus abortion and the ERA are recurring, frequent entries whereas rape and domestic violence are special issues given intense coverage.

Studies and the Women's Movement

This systematic survey of publications will be augmented by various histories and descriptions of the women's movement. In particular, books now appearing about the origins of the movement will be called upon.

Over the last 20 years a number of studies have appeared related to the women's movement. Rhetorical criticism has made some important contributions. In 1973 Karly Kohrs Campbell wrote an intriguing article exploring the contradiction inherent in women speaking at all, let alone attempting to initiate a political movement. Schaich-Hope explored the comparison of the women's liberation movement with that of the black power movement. Brenda Hancock wrote one of the first discussions of the movement in 1972. She documented the efforts at defining the "enemy." These early works made important contributions not only to rhetorical criticism but they serve to document the evolution of the movement. Yet none of these attempt to grasp the totality of the movement as it unfolds. Virtually all early studies focus on aspects of the movement. In contrast, later studies, such as that by McPherson, emphasize techniques employed by segments of the movement.[30]

Most comprehensive studies of the movement were published during the peak of activities in the mid-1970s. *Radical Feminism* by Koedt, Levine and Rapones as well as Hole and Levin's *Rebirth of Feminism* are fine studies that explore the breadth of the movement from a historical perspective. But as the movement itself progressed and diversified, writers tended to follow suit, focusing on particular issues such as rape, domestic violence, pornography, lesbians, or women in the media.

This tendency to look at aspects of the movement is highlighted by the dissertations written from 1970 to 1980. There are literally hundreds of entries over the years. Yet they fall into categories reflecting particular concerns of the movement rather than the total movement. Abortion, birth control, childbirth, media, role expectations, relationships between young and old, sex roles, self-esteem, and sexual harassment all appear. This not only reflects the vastness of the movement but on a deeper level it is illustrative of the inability or unwillingness of the women in particular to look critically at the movement. It was not until very recently with the publication of Elshtain's *Public Man and Private Woman* that we have seen any effort to conceptualize the thrust of the movement as whole, or to critically assess what it has meant. The newness of this approach is probably best illustrated by the amount of resistance Elshtain unleashed with the publication of her work.

In the course of bringing together a total perspective on the movement, these individual studies are invaluable. They provide a deepened understanding of particular issues and events. And the dissertations document the developing concerns of the movement as the topics reflect the most salient issues of the time. Thus Sharp, for instance, writing during the dominance of the woman as nigger metaphor, concentrates on the relationship of the civil rights movement to the women's movement.

Most recently, important historical retrospectives have appeared. Important among these have been Sara Evans' *Personal Politics* (1980). This book traces the origins of the movement in the early civil rights struggles. Additionally, the ever prolific Betty Friedan has offered a retrospective in *Second Stage*. These, plus the ongoing work of such leading feminists as Robin Morgan and Gloria Steinem provide a rich background within which to analyze how the movement has evolved through the images and issues addressed in the *New York Times* and *Ms.* Magazine.

While the rhetoric of the movement comes out in varied forms: speeches, talks, manifestos, books, articles and a countless variety of conversations, part of the underlying assumption here is that any social movement is necessarily concerned both with its own unity as a collective action and with explaining itself to the larger environment. Metaphors document the central thrust of both of these activities.

Conclusion

Over the two decades to be studied, then, major metaphorical constructs emerge through the rhetoric to provide the coherence and direction of the movement. The basic development of these metaphors will be charted within Griffin's overall framework of inception, rhetorical crisis, and consummation. It will be argued that each of these stages can best be understood by the emergence and subsequent shifting of dominant metaphors. These metaphors document the major ideas and strategies of the movement and establish the basis for the political struggles which unfold. In the course of these changes the movement attracts members and friends as well as creates enemies in its effort to redefine the very essence of what it means to be a woman. Each chapter will attempt to capture the metaphor as it evolves through the coverage of the women's movement in the *New York Times* and *Ms.*

The chapters will begin with an overview indicating the time period of the metaphor, its expression through the basic categories of subject of articles, roles ascribed to women, descriptive adjectives employed, political actions advocated and carried out, the justification called upon for these actions and the emerging opposition. This overview will be followed by a description and interpretation of the metaphor as it unfolds. This structure, as Griffin suggests, is intended to "preserve the idiom in which the movement was actually expressed."[31]

NOTES

1. Hannah Arendt, *On Revolution* (New York: Penquin Books, 1963), p. 46-47.

2. See Ron E. Roberts and Robert Marsh Kloss, *Social Movements: Between the Balcony and the Barricade,* Second Edition, (St. Louis: The C. V. Mosby Company, 1979), pp. 1-21 and Bernard Brock and Robert L. Scott, *Methods of Rhetorical Criticism: A Twentieth Century Perspective,* Second Edition, (Detroit: Wayne State University Press, 1980) pp. 397-400.

3. James Boggs, *Racism and the Class Struggle* (New York: Monthly Review Press, 1963), and James and Grace Lee Boggs, *Revolution and Evolution in the Twentieth Century* (New York: Monthly Review Press, 1974).

4. Leland M. Griffin, "The Rhetoric of Historical Movements," *Quarterly Journal of Speech,* 38 (April 1952), pp. 186-88. Also, Leland M. Griffin, "A Dramatistic Theory of the Rhetoric of Movements," in *Critical Responses to Kenneth Burke,* William H. Rueckert, ed., (Minneapolis: University of Minneapolis Press, 1969), pp. 456-478.

5. Leonard Binder, James Coleman, Joseph La Palombora, Lucian W. Pye, Sidney Verba and Myron Weiner, *Crises and Sequences in Political Development* (Princeton, New Jersey: Princeton University Press, 1972). Hans Toch, *The Social Psychology of Social Movements* (Indianapolis: Bobbs-Merrill, 1965). Neil J. Smelser, *Theory of Collective Behavior* (New York: The Free Press, 1962). Joseph R. Gusfield, ed., *Protest, Reform and Revolt: A Reader in Social Movements* (New York: John Wiley & Sons, Inc., 1970). Charles U. Larson, *Persuasion: Reception and Responsibility* (Belmont, California: Wadworth Publishing Company, 1973), and Nobel Books, 1951).

6. Ernest G. Bormann, "Fantasy and Rhetorical Vision: the Rhetorical Criticism of Social Reality," *Quarterly Journal of Speech,* 58 (December 1972), pp. 396-407.

38

7. Kenneth Burke, *Language as Symbolic Action: Essays on Life, Literature and Method* (Berkeley: University of California Press, 1966), pp. 52-60.

8. Herbert Blumer, "Collective Behavior" in Alfred M. Lee, ed., *New Outlines of the Principles of Sociology,* ed. 2 (1946), rev. (New York: Barnes and Noble Books, 1951).

9. For a discussion of the value assumptions underlying theoretical perspectives see Roberts and Kloss.

10. Roberts and Kloss.

11. Robert S. Cathcart, "New Approaches to the Study of Movements: Defining Movements Rhetorically," *Western Speech,* 36 (Spring 1972), pp. 82-88.

12. Eric Hoffer, *The Ordeal of Change* (New York: Harper and Row, 1964).

13. Lewis Feurer, *The Conflicts of Generations* (New York: Basic Books, Inc., 1969).

14. Toch.

15. Hadley Cantril, *The Psychology of Social Movements* (New York: John Wiley & Sons, Inc., 1941).

16. Smelser.

17. Muzafer and Carolyn W. Sherif, *Social Psychology* (New York: Harper and Row, 1969), p. 511-522.

18. Bernard Brock and Robert L. Scott, *Methods of Rhetorical Criticism: A Twentieth Century Perspective,* 2nd Edition (Detroit: Wayne State University Press, 1980), pp. 403-419.

19. Herbert W. Simons, "Requirements, Problems and Strategies: A Theory of Persuasion for Social Movements," *Quarterly Journal of Speech,* 56 (February 1970), pp. 1-11.

20. Kenneth Burke, *A Grammar of Motives* (Berkeley: University of California Press, 1970). Hugh Duncan, *Symbols in Society* (London: Oxford University Press, 1968). Peter Berger and Thomas Luckmann, *The Social Construction of Reality: A Treatise in the Sociology of Knowledge* (Garden City, New York: Doubleday & Company, Inc., 1966).

21. Peter Mitall and John P. Hewitt, "The Quasi-Theory of Confrontations and the Management of Dissent," *Social Problems,* 18, No. 1, 1970, p. 17-26.

22. Michael Osborn, "Archetypal Metaphor in Rhetoric: The Light-Dark Family," *The Quarterly Journal of Speech,* 53 (April 1967), pp. 115-26.

23. Edwin Black, "The Second Persona," *Quarterly Journal of Speech,* 56 (April 1970), pp. 109-119. Kathleen Hall Jamieson, "The Metaphoric Cluster in the Rhetoric of Pope Paul VI and Edmund G. Brown, Jr.," *Quarterly Journal of Speech,* 66 (February 1980), pp. 51-72.

Vernon Jenson, "British Views on the Eve of the American Revolution: Trapped by the Family Metaphor," *Quarterly Journal of Speech,* 63 (February 1977), p. 43-50. Michael Osborn, "Archetypal Metaphors in Rhetoric: The Light-Dark Family," *Quarterly Journal of Speech,* 53 (April 1967), pp. 115-26 and "The Evolution of the Archetypal Sea in Rhetoric and Poetic," *Quarterly Journal of Speech,* 63 (December 1977), p. 347-63.

24. Kenneth Burke, *Attitudes Toward History* (Boston: Beacon Press, 1955), p. 213.

25. J. David Sapir and J. Christopher Crocker, *The Social Use of Metaphor: Essays on the Anthropology of Rhetoric* (Pennsylvania: University of Pennsylvania Press, 1977).

26. George Lakoff and Mark Johnson, *Metaphors We Live By* (Chicago: University of Chicago Press, 1980).

27. The controversy was recently addressed in a special edition of *Central States Speech Journal,* Volume 31 (Winter 1980), devoted to an exploration of the "state of the art."

28. The issue of public and private is extraordinarily complex. Some of the most important contributions in understanding these concepts have come from the works of Hannah Arendt and, more recently, those of Jeane Bethke Elshtain, especially *Public Man Private Woman* (Princeton: Princeton University Press, 1981). Both Arendt and Elshtain take a particularly rhetorical stance in their discussions of political philosophy. A forceful plea for a reexamination of these political categories by rhetorical criticism was offered by S. Michael Halloran in "Public vs. Private: Richard Sennett on Public Life and Authority," *Quarterly Journal of Speech,* 67 (August 1981), p. 322. An earlier elaboration can be found in the comments of Lloyd Bitzer, "Rhetoric and Public Knowledge," in Don Burke, editor, *Rhetoric, Philosophy and Literature: An Exploration* (West Lafayette, Indiana: University Press, 1978).

29. Leland M. Griffin, "On Studying Movements," *Central States Speech Journal,* 31 (Winter 1980), pp. 223-232.

30. Karlyn Kohrs Campbell, "The Rhetoric of Women's Liberation: An Oxymoron," *Quarterly Journal of Speech,* 59 (February 1973), pp. 74-86. Brenda Robinson Hancock, "Affirmation by Negation in the Women's Liberation Movement," *Quarterly Journal of Speech,* 58 (October 1972), pp. 264-271. Louise McPhersen, "Communication Techniques of the Women's Liberation Front," *Today's Speech,* Vol. 21, No. 2, Spring 1973. Diane Schaich-Hope, "Redefinition of Self: A Comparison of the Rhetoric of the Women's Liberation Movement and Black Liberation Movements," *Today's Speech,* (Winter 1975), pp. 20-21.

31. Griffin, 1952, p. 187.

CHAPTER III

Inception:
Woman as Nigger

The Woman as Nigger metaphor emerged with the inception of the movement. Beginning in the early 1960s this metaphor focused the movement until 1968 when it was no longer able to either unify women or to attract support from the larger environment. The metaphor was marked by the prevalence of terms employed by the *New York Times* drawn directly from the civil rights struggle to describe the condition of women, the major actors and the activities of the movement. Ti-Grace Atkinson, for example, was the "new Malcolm X" and Betty Friedan the "female Martin Luther King." Women were described with adjectives such as "second class citizens," "minority group" or were overtly referred to as being treated "like Negroes." Virtually all of the political activity during this period was justified by reference to the civil rights struggle and the strategies and tactics were parallel. Demonstrations, sit-ins, pickets and efforts to organize among the "grass roots" were the most important actions taken.

Opposition to the movement was unorganized but consistent. It generally took the form of laughter or ridicule. Even the tone of much of the reporting of public demonstrations often reflected the somewhat amused stance of the *New York Times* in the early years.

The Recognition of the Problem

The metaphor was initially articulated within the radical community in the early 1960s but by 1968 it was consistently employed by and attached to the more liberal feminists. By 1968, for example, NOW was almost routinely referred to as "the NAACP for women."

In the course of this metaphor, women began the process of questioning their identity. They recognized that there was something very wrong with their role and status in society. It was through the comparison of their condition with that of the African-American that they were able to question the prevailing definition of women. Long thought to have occupied a privileged and comfortable position within the society, it was only by recognizing the similarity in their condition with that of African-Americans that women were able to give voice and direction to the uneasiness that had been growing in them for many years. The recognition that women had been paternalized, treated as second class citizens and unable to be seen as autonomous, independent adults fueled the early formation of the movement. In these early years women had no sense of their own worth as human beings, but they had come to recognize they would no longer tolerate the lack of worth made so clear by the contrast between their own condition and that of African-Americans. Like the African-American, women were no longer content to be "outsiders."

The purpose of this chapter is to describe the development of this metaphor as portrayed through the coverage of women in the *New York Times*. With the emergence and development of the metaphor the movement began to take shape and become a part of American political life.

The Quiet Beginning

Our image of social movements has been profoundly affected by the French and Russian revolutions. We envision throngs of people streaming through the streets. These images have become as much a part of our theoretical perspectives as they have of the popular folklore. As a result, we tend to think of revolutions or social movements as having precise beginning and ending points. This is no less true of rhetorical criticism than it is of political science or history. Griffin, whose work has helped to initiate and shape the study of social movements, reflects this when he defines the point of inception as being established when an individual or group steps forward with a resounding No! to the way things are. He argues that:

> Movements begin when some pivotal individuals or group...suffering attitudes of alienation in a given social system, and drawn (consciously or unconsciously) by the impious dream of a mythic order...enact, give voice to a No.[1]

In reality of course this kind of dramatic naysaying is only made possible by the countless small changes in the lives of hundreds of thousands of individuals. Changes which have come together to finally compel people to think and act in new and different ways. The contemporary women's movement is no exception to this.

Rather than beginning with a forceful no!, it started with

a quiet hmm...as the very nature of the American Woman was called into question by the extraordinary developments in the lives of all Americans following the end of World War II.

The "American Woman" has certainly changed over time. But prior to WWII, women's lives were fairly clearly defined and confined within the private, domestic realm. While women had always provided labor for the growing mills and factories in America, it was not until World War II that thousands of women poured out of the home and into the factories and offices that had once been the almost exclusive domain of men. With the end of the war men not only returned home, they returned to their work. Women, again by the thousands, were suddenly no longer needed in the plants and industries. For some, this was a welcome relief. But for many others, expanded and enlarged by the sense of themselves as competent workers as well as mothers, daughters and wives, "returning to the home" was met with anger, frustration and in some instances protest. Rosie the Riveter was never going to be quite the same again.

This new-found experience in the labor force was coupled with an explosion of consumer items and technological advances that lessened women's responsibilities within the home. Advanced washing machines, vacuum cleaners and a host of "labor saving" appliances along with prepared foods diminished the sense of importance women gained from their responsibilities. Additionally, the technology actually lessened much of the difficult and time consuming work of maintaining a household. Women in virtually all social classes in both urban and rural areas began to find themselves less occupied and fulfilled by their contribution in making a home and raising a family.

Throughout the 1950s women felt themselves becoming less important or useful. More and more they were seen as simply consumers or ornaments. While sometimes packaged in a glamorous image, the reality behind the gloss was one of a slowly eroding world in which women had always made their most important contributions—the home and family.[3]

With the beginning of the 1960s the glitter surrounding women had begun to tarnish. A full scale debate surfaced over the very nature of women.

By 1961 this debate found its way to the pages of the *New York Times*. Here the clash between the old and the new concepts of women were summarized in articles pondering the biological nature of women. On one side, authors pointed out that women were born to be wives and mothers. They harkened back to her role as keeper of the "civic virtues."[4] Yet as demand for workers increased across the country and as more and more women received advanced education, others began to argue that women were capable of life outside the home. Women who spent their lives totally within the domestic realm were beginning to be seen as a "waste of a precious resource."[5] Passing on civic virtues within the confines of the home was simply no longer enough. Efforts to bring the two sides of the debate together resulted in curious metaphors. Young, educated women returning to the home to become wives and mothers were compared to living lives like plants without water— becoming all "vegetation without flowers."[6]

As women experienced an increased necessity to contribute outside of the home, they also expressed a desire to change their status within the home as well. Marriage was to become a full "partnership."[7] The meaning of this concept was always vague, but the dissatisfaction it represented was not.

The growing uncertainty and ambiguity around the role of women was signalled by the convening of a special Presidential Commission appointed by President Kennedy. While no doubt reflecting the tensions around the role of women, the establishment of the commission created something less than a stir. In fact, in Kennedy's subsequent State of the Nation Address, he made no reference to women. When a female journalist raised this omission at the following press conference, she was greeted with outright laughter. While a troubling issue, the role of women was hardly a matter for serious politics.[8]

Also like other revolutions and social movements, change and uncertainty are not enough to bring masses of people to action. The change has to be interpreted and explained in a political context. This was made possible by the women involved in the early days of the civil rights movement. It was during the course of these struggles in the south that women not only saw themselves as political actors but developed a vocabulary to explain and interpret their own lives and experiences in a political framework.

Early Roots in the Civil Rights Movement

In many ways the roots of the contemporary women's movement are deep in the south in the hesitant questioning begun by those women who had been actively involved in the civil rights struggles in the late 1950s and early 1960s. Black and white women, motivated by concepts of social justice, a belief in the ability of people to create a better future and the confidence that they could develop a more human society, plunged into the heart of these political struggles. Often risking family and friends, black and white women became active participants with SNCC, CORE and SCLC as well as a host of religious and campus based organizations. During the course of these struggles women became aware of themselves as political actors and acquired a framework within which to confront their own oppression.

Yet neither the condition of women inside these organizations nor the nature of their oppression was immediately clear. While obviously absent from the strategic and theoretical leadership during this period, women none-theless were able to participate in some of the most impor-tant aspects of political activity on a near equal basis. Mass demonstrations, marches, sit-ins and voter registration drives were all opportunities for women, along with men, to experience a new sense of themselves as political actors.[9]

It was through these activities that women became familiar with a political vocabulary that enabled them to clarify relationships they had understood to be destructive for both blacks and whites. Exploitation, oppression, powerlessness, and second class citizenship all became powerful concepts defining and challenging social ar-rangements they had been taught to think of as normal and natural. It was through these conceptualizations that women were able to recognize the parallel between the relationships between the races and the interactions they were experien-cing with men. This recognition of their own "oppression" was coupled with a growing understanding of themselves as political people who had learned the importance of col-lective struggle.

Thus, it was out of the initial recognition of the disparity between what they were fighting *for* and what they—as black and white women—were experiencing in the course of these struggles that women began to raise the first quiet questions.

As Sara Evans so clearly points out, this initial ques-tioning was almost a parody on the general condition of women. It was in the corridors of SNCC, an organization dependent heavily on the work of women, that the first fram-ing of women's issues was advanced. For the November 1964 staff retreat in Waveland, Mississippi the SNCC Position Paper, Women in the Movement, appeared on a crowded agenda with the following note: authors names withheld by request.

This anonymity reflected the fear and powerlessness women felt. In these early days women had not yet found

48

their own voice. Nor were they ready to stand up publicly for their own feelings and perceptions. As the authors of the position paper argued in defense of their decision to be unidentified:

> Think about the kinds of things the authors, if made known, would have to suffer because of raising this kind of discussion. Nothing so final as...outright exclusion, but the kinds of things which are killing to the insides—insinuations, ridicule, over-exaggerated compensation.[10]

Within this hesitant almost apologetic questioning and struggling to understand what they were thinking and feeling, we see the development of the first metaphor—woman as nigger. Only by drawing on the analogy of the experience of racism and the status of blacks were women able to gain insight into their own condition.

Woman as Nigger

Woman as nigger developed first within the radical community as a way to define the experiences of women within the movement as well as within the larger society.

The justification for raising the issue of women's place came not from any new conceptualization of women or their political responsibility, but from the *contrast* between the status of women within the movement and the principles of the movement itself. This disparity provided a basis for questioning the existing definition of women. But as yet there was no new sense of an independent female identity.

The metaphor became a powerful foundation from which to articulate the position of women. It drew upon the legitimacy of the civil rights struggle and the energy created by that movement. Throughout the early 1960s it extended beyond the radical community and more and more was used to characterize the position of women in society. We even find the *George Washington Law Review,* not exactly a radical publication, containing an article articulating the accepted parallel:

> Discriminatory attitudes toward women are strikingly parallel to those regarding Negroes. Women have experienced both subtle and explicit forms of discrimination comparable to the inequalities imposed upon minorities. Contemporary scholars have been impressed by the interrelation of these two problems in the United States, whether their point of departure has been a study of women or of racial theories.[11]

Or more simply, Betty Friedan began NOW with the idea it would be an "NAACP for women."[12]

The development of this metaphor as the initial conceptualization of the movement justified for women a struggle for themselves, even though they did not think of themselves as being particularly worthy human beings, except by contrast.

The civil rights premise provided an initial basis for unity among the members. Not exactly known for its unified concepts, the political "left" had already achieved some measure of agreement on the importance of civil rights. Likewise a greater and greater portion of the American people were being drawn into the belief that there was something fundamentally wrong in the way the relationships between human beings had developed in this country.

Development in the New York Times

This metaphor appears first in the *New York Times* as

the sole justification for considering the condition of women throughout the early and mid-1960s. As the movement began to grow, the basic function of metaphor, to explain the "new" in terms of the "familiar," comes into play. The major actors of the movement begin to be described in terms of known civil rights leaders. And the public actions they initiate draw their validity from the actual strategies of the civil rights struggle. Ultimately the metaphor provides a basis by which women can conceive of themselves as a collective group. Only after they had made this leap would they begin to explore a deeper sense of their own identity.

Using the conceptual vocabulary of prejudice, discrimination and subjugation, letters and articles appear to contrast the concern for civil rights with a concern for the rights of women. Significantly, it is this contrast which provides the only justification for concern. The contrast first appears in a letter in early January criticizing John Kennedy's State of the Nation Address. Pointing out that the address had placed a heavy emphasis on civil rights, the author goes on to argue that there was no mention of equal rights for women. She explains that:

> Women—that large segment of the population as much in need of consideration as those with which Kennedy expressed such concern—were not even mentioned.[13]

Thus the metaphor begins with the premise that in the discussion of civil rights—women are being left out. Reporting on the status of women at the beginning of the "space age" Lee Graham documents this voice:

> Racial prejudice has certainly received its share of analysis but...prejudice on the basis of sex has been largely neglected up to now.[14]

It is this theme of "omission" that gives the metaphor its original base.

On a descriptive level the vast majority of adjectives in the early 1960s continue the traditional stereotypes. Women are portrayed as less dependable, changing, and, if more intelligent than men, wise enough to "soft pedal their mental capacity." Without ever directly challenging these descriptions, there is the recognition of a growing discontent with the gilded lot.[15]

Significantly, in 1962 we also see the first conscious application of terms directly from the civil rights struggle surfacing to describe women. Women begin to be classed as "second class citizens" and termed a "political minority."

Yet throughout the early 1960s, the leading controversy is not over the political and social status of women. It remains over her biological and natural role. The discontent in women which was clearly acknowledged was attributed as much to her inability to balance her time properly or to the inability to "get good help" as anything else.

Graham's article which pointed out the limitations of women in the new "space age" sparked a flurry of letters. These letters basically reaffirmed the prevailing myths of the unsuitability of women for public or professional life. And they also foreshadowed one of the most powerful arguments to later be levied against the ERA. Somehow the question of equality for women evoked the response—"Are they ready to be soldiers?" The responsibilities of citizenship and public life are equated with the last male line of defense, the willingness to engage in military combat.[16]

But in the early 1960s this is a seldom mentioned question. The issue of women is generally treated with a degree of lightness amid the food, fashions, and furnishing articles. Yet there is a growing note of unrest. In September of 1962 this unrest is focussed in a review of *Her Infinite Variety: The American Women as Lover, Mate and Rival.* The review summarizes the book as trying to:

...find out what makes the modern, educated, middle class American Woman discontented with her gilded lot, for it has been obvious for some time—Pearl Buck, for one, was writing about it a quarter of a century ago—that emancipated woman is dissatisfied.[17]

By 1963 the debate over the biological nature of women disappears. It is now accepted that the working mother and working wife are a part of American life. And the seriousness of the discontent replaces the efforts to simply dismiss it as frivolous. In fact we begin to see an explicit connection being made between the efforts of black Americans and the struggles of women. It is this comparison which launches the seriousness with which women should be considered. In a speech before the International Council of Women the Assistant Secretary of Labor, Ester Peterson, is reported to stress the parallel between the current civil rights struggles and the efforts of women to achieve full partnership in the affairs of the nation. Peterson says:

Thoughtful persons are beginning to see that discrimination against minority groups is wasteful of human resources and is a check upon the full realization of our nation's potential. Similar recognition is being given to potential of our women power.[18]

Thus in 1963 as women within SNCC were meeting to form their position paper and the *Feminine Mystique* was rolling off the presses, there is a growing recognition of the parallel conditions of blacks and women. The metaphor begins to illuminate the unknown world of women by drawing upon the known world of the black struggle.

This metaphor is of course fraught with contradictions. One of the most striking arises from the concept of women as a political minority. The term is applied so frequently it comes as almost a surprise to women to find that they were actually a majority. This is resolved by expanding the description to read "a minority group that is actually a majority."[19]

By 1964 the earlier emphasis on women in the home has been totally replaced by the desire to find ways to "balance responsibilities." Women are beginning to appear in public roles and Lady Bird Johnson introduces her series of luncheons for women "doers."[20]

And in 1964 we have the passage of the Civil Rights Act which codified the struggles waged by black Americans. Women were included as part of the language of this act as a joke. Even this did not provide much activity on the part of women. Along with the minimal concern for the Civil Rights Act, women were equally silent on a UN resolution that year. The UN proposed to outlaw genocide, forced labor and the subjugation of women. While endorsing the outlawing of genocide and slavery, the United States took the position that forced labor and the subjugation of women were "domestic affairs" which should be left up to the decisions of nations. They should not be discussed by international bodies. This entire debate and discussion, as well as the U.S. vote against the provisions in 1967 was conducted with barely a letter of protest from women.[21] But such a protest would have required a level of consciousness of their own identity beyond that of comparison.

Perhaps most revealing of the concept of the female identity was in an exchange of articles between Malcolm Bradbury and Gloria Steinem. Bradbury in "American Women Are Rude," evokes just about every stereotypical and degrading image of women imaginable. Characterizing women as gossiping, mindless and shrieking, Bradbury paints the picture of women as the object of an American man's money in much the same way that the English spend money on their dogs. This less than flattering article is responded to by Gloria Steinem. Steinem, entitling her article "Visiting Englishmen Are No Bed of Roses" launches a playful attack on the Englishman visiting the colonies. Throughout the article it is clear that Steinem feels she has absolutely no basis by which to refute any of Bradbury's comments about women. The sense of a human identity, worthy of respect and offended by the kind of jokes and comments that would be easily labeled as racist if applied to blacks, is totally absent at this point.[22]

A Turning Point

After the Civil Rights Act, however, the joke of including sex discrimination in the language of the law begins to be a focal point for political action. By 1965 we see not only an increase in the coverage of court battles being fought for and by women, but the first reports of their "militant protests."[23] All of this activity continues to be justified and described in terms drawn directly from the civil rights movement.

The political implications of the changing activities of women begin to be discussed in the extreme terms. Lady Bird Johnson in a commencement address takes the opportunity to welcome the "women's revolution"—a loaded term given the political context of the mid-1960s. And the intellectual community begins a much more serious dialogue about the role of women. In an insightful review "After Nora Slammed the Door: American women in the 1960s—the Unfinished Revolution" the battle to overcome second class citizenship is portrayed. Drawing on the work of de Beauvoir and Friedan, the author raises the first indictment of the role of the housewife. No longer simply raising the question of the balancing of time between home and career, Merriman actually ponders if the role of housewife could ever be fulfilling in and of itself. This questioning is greeted by the reviewer with a sense of shock and the fear that despite its many good qualities, the book might stir up "guilt feelings" in the readers.[24]

Thus women's political activity begins to be described in terms heretofor reserved for the civil rights struggle. The attack on the family begins to be "revolutionary," while the questioning of women's roles, "militant." In a report on the meeting of the Lucy Stone League, we find "female voices were raised in militant protest against social and business inequities."[25] At this point the metaphor is expanded. It shifts from using civil rights as a justification for tactics and becomes descriptive of the tactics themselves. The public, political actions of women become explained by the adjectives of the civil rights struggle.

Also during this period the first significant splitting away from the biological definition of women occurs. In a review of *The Love Fraud* by Elizabeth Janeway entitled "A Search for Values" there is the first break with the biologically accepted identity of women. For the first time, childbearing is cast as a purely biological function, separate and apart from a "career." Having rejected the role of women as totally biologically determined, women open up a host of questions about how they have been shaped by the political and cultural world.[26] Using the vocabulary of "second class citizens," "oppressed people" and "exploitation," women began to explore their role in the larger society arguing that both the biological and political definition of their being is insufficient.

The Emerging Opposition

The escalation of struggle by women resulted in an increase in the attacks on the movement. Laughter and scorn were coupled with direct challenges to the feminist position and the attribution of curious motives to the women involved in putting them forward. And, as becomes characteristic of the attackers, they are often other women. Typical of this kind of attack was that in "Feminine Mystique Under Fire." Here the *Times* reports on a speech delivered by Jo Foxworth, a woman vice president of an advertising firm. In a speech before a professional association she wins the approval of her male colleagues by challenging Ms. Friedan to a debate on the grounds that the *Feminine Mystique* is a "mistaque." The tone of Ms. Foxworth's statements could be captured in the phrase current pre-women's liberation—catty. She describes Friedan:

> Miss Friedan juices up her typewriter with saltwater tears and a splash of vitroil and proceeds to slosh out some really heart rending laments for the entire female sex....[27]

Thus Foxworth becomes an archetype of one of the most persistent problems to plague the movement, criticism of the movement and denial of its validity by other women who have achieved "success" within the male world, playing by male rules. For unlike the black movement, the most effective critics were members of the collective group.

But the intensity of the criticism was not reserved for only the public or visible feminist. In August of 1965 the President's Commission on the Status of Women published its report. The report covered four years of intense research under two presidents. Edited by Margaret Mead and Francis Kaplan, the introduction to the massive document terms it "an invitation to action." Chronicling the dismal economic, political and social status of women, the report attempted to be totally descriptive rather than to advocate "feminist ideas." However, it was greeted by outright attack. Edward Eddy's review in the *Times* is a sample of the reaction:

> Is this the cry of the militant female, rising again

in her wrath, setting down once more for all to ponder the demands of her disadvantaged self?...Or is it merely the final gasp of the feminist movement, which will be done in by its own self-righteousness because it cannot stand the inevitable snicker and snort?[28]

On the Move

Despite the attempt to dismiss the report, its disturbing picture of the life of the American woman lent a legitimacy to the stresses and strains that women had been feeling. And the movement was accelerated toward visible, vocal political activity. The temper of the times was captured in the extraordinary number of articles discussing and analyzing the "modern woman." No longer seen as the passive, delicate young or old thing, women were described as "getting into everything." During this period of intense activity the metaphor with civil rights became solidified as the justification for action. It is used to describe the public and private activities of women and is consciously employed by them as they not only become more politically active but as they expand into the "untraditional job."[29]

The very nature of their political activity helps to build the metaphor. Using the Civil Rights Act, women press their demands on a variety of legal fronts. Fred Graham observes this when he comments on the "incidental benefits" of the act:

The Negro Civil Rights movement has incidentally benefited several other minority groups, Mexican Americans, Puerto Ricans and American Indians. It has also produced surprising dividends for a majority group—women.[30]

On a more subtle level the metaphor takes on an almost tangible form. Much of the activity under the Act was a direct challenge to a host of discriminatory state laws. Out of these activities emerge what came to be called the "all purpose plaintiff, the negro woman."[31]

The Development of NOW

Much of this activity in the legal arena was the direct result of the National Organization of Women created by Betty Friedan. Friedan and the early founders thought of NOW as a revolutionary step toward progress. It was established to fight for the "true equality for all women in America...as a part of the worldwide revolution in human rights now taking place."[32] Yet it was not the worldwide revolution which gave NOW its status within the U.S. Rather, over and over again, both the press and its own directors simply called it "the NAACP for women." NOW not only used the civil rights metaphor to describe itself, but it also framed its arguments based on the already accepted premises granted to black Americans. Drawing on the contrast between the acceptance of the injustice of racial discrimination, NOW urged President Johnson to encourage the Equal Employment Opportunities Commission to be more vigorous on behalf of women. They argued in a public letter to Johnson:

> ...[there seems to be a] reluctance among some of its male employees (EEOC) to combat sex discrimination as vigorously as they seek to combat racial discrimination.[33]

NOW and a host of small radical groups began to form to further explore the condition of women. Their emphasis was almost totally directed toward developing forums for education, raising the demand for day care and the desire to enforce minimum wage laws for women. Counselling centers and women's networks were established.

In the course of this very real class and racial divisions began to surface. But as becomes characteristic of the movement, they are rarely confronted. With over 2/3 of all families headed by women living in poverty and with domestic service still being the primary work available to minority women both Betty Friedan and Clare Booth Luce, two women who rarely agreed, urge their followers to try and find good "domestic help as a way to cope with their burdens."[34]

On the Streets

The troubling division of race and class were swept aside as the movement burst out of the home and on to the streets. No longer just using the language and legitimacy of the civil rights movement, women adopted its more radical strategies.

By 1968 all of this action was summarized in a *New York Times* article announcing the "Second Feminist Wave." Bradley's hope that the militancy of women would simply die out was swamped under a flurry and fury of activity.

Under the leadership of the radical women, pickets, protests and disruptions of the most imaginative and humorous sorts appeared regularly. Reaching the cover of the Magazine section, the *Times* queries, "What do women want?" Picturing young women, looking for all the world as though they should be at home watching their children or sitting quietly behind the typewriter, the article captured the emerging anger of women. Pictures reveal women clutching large picket signs with slogans reading:

Women can think as well as type.

It's a woman's civil right to bear only wanted
children.
Give women a chance at better jobs![35]

The EEOC became a favorite spot for demonstrations.
Women routinely attended the hearings of the commission
on sex discrimination (which had no women members) and
managed to make enough noise to get themselves arrested
and thrown out.[36]

Stretching of the Metaphor

It was during these militant activities that the metaphor
Woman as Nigger was further extended from the political
sphere into the home. The sophisticated intellectual questioning of the role of women as wife and mother was lost
in the equation of marriage with slavery. Placards began
to appear with the legend: A chicken in every pot/A whore
in every home! Thus the metaphor, powerful in creating unity when applied to the political sphere, raised a troubling
and divisive issue when applied to the home.[37] But the limitations of analogy and the theoretical issues raised by the extension of the metaphor were drowned out by this stepped
up action. Newspapers were picketed for job discrimination
based on listing jobs under help wanted—male or female.
Airlines were charged with both age and sex discrimination.
And the legalization of abortion became an important arena
for political action.

The civil rights metaphor not only fueled these activities, it helped to intimidate the opposition. "Aunt Toms"
were identified and the use of "girl" was equated with "boy".
Emerging feminist leaders were described in terms of their
civil rights counter parts. Florynce Henderson becomes the
H. Rap Brown of the movement and Ti-Grace Atkinson
became the female voice of black power.[38]

Slavery in the Home

The troublesome aspects of the analogy continue to surface. Proving itself so powerful in generating action, the Woman as Nigger provided one of the core touchstones of emerging feminist theory. Ti-Grace, who was noted as the theoretical leader of the more radical New York women articulated the basic analysis:

> The institution of marriage has the same effects the institution of slavery has. It separates people in the same category, disperses them, keeps them from identifying as a class. The masses of slaves didn't recognize their condition, either. To say that a woman is really "happy" with her home and kids is irrelevant as saying that the blacks were happy being taken care of by old massa. She is defined by her maintenance role as her husband's defined by his productive role.[39]

As the metaphor takes shape in the private realm, then, early feminist theory began to equate the family with slavery. The raising of children became a form of bondage. This image surfaced again and again to haunt the movement. Ultimately it became one of the most difficult and troubling aspects of the entire struggle. But at this stage, the extension of the metaphor seemed only "natural."

As a result of this initial probing opened up by the metaphor, women saw themselves as engaging in a struggle to expand the definition of humanness. There was little sense that important human values loaded with class and racial distinctions, were being discarded. Rather women were seeing themselves only as attacking that which was destructive. We find a simple statement of the goals:

We want to get away from relating to men merely as sex objects. We believe in a total change in the social structure so that men and women will be free to come together in a more meaningful relationship.[40]

This kind of lofty goal, however, was quickly put in its proper place by those who recognized the real threat implied to the stability of society by the effort to explore the role of women. Men, and many women, responded with a rather direct "oh come off it, why ruin it for the rest of us?"[41]

By 1968, then, the metaphor had solidified and become a natural part of the description of the condition of women. It was constantly called upon to justify action and to provide a source of strategies. The ease with which the metaphor was employed is revealed in a book review by Gloria Steinem. She writes:

In fact, women who write, like Negroes who write, are supposed to be specialists on themselves, and little else.

And later:

Born Female is enough to convince anyone literate, from male chauvinist to female Uncle Tom, that superstitions and restrictive prejudices on which our system is built are depriving the country of nearly half its talent.

And finally she points out:

...in a very quiet and liberating way, Caroline Bird is something of a Malcolm X for women, but Malcolm X just before he died when he had developed beyond anti-white feelings.[42]

Wall Street Woman

As the feminist movement continued to intrude into virtually every area of life, reactions took a number of forms. Perhaps the epitome of the retrenchment and retreat on the part of males was the phenomenon of the Wall Street Sweater Girl. During two heady weeks in September of 1968 the usually sedate and conservative Wall Street was turned into a sea of gawkers at a young secretary. As many as 10,000 men gathered at the gates of the subway to catch a glimpse of the woman. This overt attack on a single, rather shy young woman as nothing more than an object to be looked at, went strikingly unnoticed by feminists.[43] But in a short period of time, this action as well as the thousands of unsuspecting young men on street corners who ventured a whistle or the sophisticated judges of the Miss America Pageant, all came under direct assault. Women took their revenge for the wall street woman.

The Breakdown

The political climate in 1968 was extremely intense. There were rebellions in major cities, assassinations, elections, violence and the Vietnam War. All of this led the *Times* to devote an entire article to the "Equality Revolution" by Herbert Gans. Gans looked at the movements of the period and argued that they were an effort to gain equality in the economic, social and political spheres.[44] The article provoked an angry reply from Karen De Crow, later to become President of New York NOW. De Crow offered the first real statement of the need for women to be seen as having their own separate identity. She avoided the contrast with blacks and simply demanded that women themselves begin to define who they are and what they want. She writes:

Gans practically ignored the group in America which is both the poorest and the most unequal: women. In 144 column inch article, 2½ inches are devoted to women who comprise 51% of the population...but my protest is not over the quantity but the content.

In the 2½ inches the reader is informed that (1) men sometimes do housework, and (2) women are now having orgasms. Well exquisite though the pleasures of an orgasm and cozy though it is too have someone doing the dishes, I must speak out as a woman and say this is not enough. It is time sociologist authors recognize it...Although men have come into the house...women simply have not come out.[45]

Through the political activity and organization that women had generated from the early 1960s a new image of themselves was slowly taking shape. The Woman as Nigger metaphor had enabled women to think and act in ways that opened up a vision of themselves as political actors. And in the course of the very activity that this contrast posed, it became insufficient. By acknowledging exploitation and subjugation women were able to see they were not only second class citizens but they had been turned into objects in both the public and private realm. Thus the metaphor provided the intellectual foundation for the development of the next stage in the evolution of the female identity, the Woman as Object.

At the same time, however, the Woman as Nigger metaphor was not without its contradictions. It also laid the foundation for the basic notion that the role of women as human beings was incompatible with their responsibilities inside a family. In addition it obscured two increasingly pressing dimensions of reality: the racism of white women and the very real class distinctions that were emerging.

Catherine Stimpson notes the inability of the analogy to continue to stretch to cover the growing racial tensions.

> ...the analogy evades, in the rhetorical haze, the harsh fact of white women's racism...the racism of white women dictates more than a desire to dominate something; it also bears on her participation in what Eldridge Cleaver calls the 'funky facts of life.'[46]

The alliance between black and white women, born out of the recognition of their common oppression within the movement could not long overshadow class and social differences. With the emerging black consciousness, black women began to articulate the limitations of the "sisterhood." Linda La Rue, writing in the *Black Scholar* points out the shortcoming:

> Common oppression is fine for rhetoric, but it does not reflect the actual distance between the oppression of the black man and woman who are unemployed and the 'oppression' of the American white woman who is 'sick and tired' of Playboy foldouts.[47]

Thus the very concept which gave the metaphor its initial power—the black/white analogy—became the element which ultimately forced women to abandon it. As racial tensions escalated in the late 1960s the metaphor seemed strangely out of date. It lost its ability to define the legitimacy of the movement or to attract people to it. It fell out of use as the reality it helped to define changed.

NOTES

1. Griffin, 1952, pp. 184–188.

2. Majorie Rosen, "Popcorn Venus or How the Movies Made Women Smaller than Life," *Ms.*, April 1974, pp. 41-46.

3. Rothman, pp. 177-211.

4. "Pope Stresses Dignity of Women," *New York Times,* 7 September 1961, p. 7.

5. Mary Bunting, "A Huge Waste: Educated Womanpower," *New York Times,* 7 May 1961, p. 23.

6. Ibid.

7. Emma Harrison, "Dr. Mead Says Battle of Sexes Is Outdated by Modern World," *New York Times,* 13 October 1961, p. 37.

8. "A Chivalrous Kennedy Backs Women's Rights," *New York Times,* 9 November 1961, p. 14.

9. Evans, pp. 5-40.

10. Evans, p. 223.

11. Hope, p. 19.

12. Betty Friedan, *It Changed My Life* (New York: Dell Publishing Company, Inc., 1977), p. 23.

13. "Equal Rights for Woman Urged", *New York Times,* 17 January 1962, p. 32.

14. Lee Graham, "Who's in Charge Here?—Not Women!", *New York Times,* 2 September 1962, p. 8.

15. Hodding Carter, "Yes Tennessee, There Are Southern Belles," *New York Times,* 7 October 1962, VI, p. 32-33.

16. "Letters: 'Who's in Charge' by Lee Graham," *New York Times,* 16 September 1962, VI, p. 22.

17. Nina Epton, "Review Her Infinite Variety: The American Woman as Lover, Mate and Rival," *New York Times,* 20 September 1962, VII, p. 20.

18. "Civil Rights Linked to Women's Goals," *New York Times,* 25 June 1963, p. 13.

19. Majorie Hunter, "US Panel Urges Women to Sue for Equal Rights," *New York Times,* 12 October 1963, p. 1.

20. "Miss Hayes Guest of Mrs. Johnson," *New York Times,* 17 January 1964, p. 22.

21. Fred P. Graham, "Bar Unit Neutral on UN Treaties," *New York Times,* 29 April 1967, p. 13 and "Anti-Slavery Accord Ratified by Senate," *New York Times,* 3 November 1967, p. 5.

22. Malcolm Bradbury, "American Women Are Rude," *New York Times,* 29 March 1964, VI, p. 48, and Gloria Steinem, "Visiting Englishmen Are No Bed of Roses," *New York Times,* 29 March 1964, VI, p. 49.

23. McCandlish Phillips, "A Mrs. Is a Miss in Lucy Stone League," *New York Times,* 15 January 1965, p. 17.

24. Beverly Grunwald, "After Nora Slammed the Door: American Women in the 1960s—the Unfinished Revolution," *New York Times,* 9 August 1964, p. 14, VII.

25. Phillips.

26. Elizabeth Janeway, "A Search for Values," *New York Times,* 28 March 1965, VII, p. 14.

27. Walter Carlson, "Advertising: Feminine Mystique Under Fire," *New York Times,* 20 June 1965, p. 46.

28. Edward Eddy, "On Being Female," *New York Times,* 1 August 1965, VII, p. 6.

29. Elizabeth Janeway, "A Woman's Role—Is Many Things," *New York Times,* 1 August 1965, VII, p. 6. Also, "Firebells Ahead?," *New York Times,* 9 February 1966, p. 41.

30. Fred Graham, "The Law: Rights Case Yields Dividends for Woman," *New York Times,* 13 February 1966, IV, p. 8.

31. Ibid., p. 8.

32. Lisa Hamnel, "They Met in Victorian Parlor to Demand 'True Equality'—NOW," *New York Times,* 22 November 1966, p. 44.

33. Ibid.

34. "For Divorced Wives Alimony or Severance Pay?" *New York Times,* 22 March 1967, p. 34.

35. Martha Weinman Lear, "The Second Feminist Wave," *New York Times,* 20 March 1968, VI, p. 24.

36. Ibid.

37. Ibid.

38. Ibid., p. 50.

39. Ibid.

40. Ibid.

41. "NOW and Never," *New York Times,* 31 March 1968, VI, p. 14.

42. Gloria Steinem, " 'Anonymous' Was a Woman," *New York Times,* 11 August 1968, VII, p. 8.

43. "10,000 Wait in Vain for Appearance of Wall Street Sweater Girl," *New York Times,* 21 September 1968, p. 14.

44. Herbert J. Gans, "The 'Equality' Revolution," *New York Times,* 3 November 1968, VI, p. 36.

45. "Letters," *New York Times,* 24 November 1968, VI, p. 88.

46. Hope, p. 19.
47. Ibid.

CHAPTER IV
The Woman As Object

By the end of the 1960s, the Woman as Nigger metaphor was no longer able to provide unity to the movement. The reality of the rebellions in Watts, Detroit and other major cities across the nation attested to the growing racial antagonisms inside the nation. Violence and fear overshadowed the images evoked by the early hopeful days of the civil rights movement. The rise of Black Power, black nationalism and the separatist tendencies within the movement resulted in the civil rights struggle becoming a source of intense division. Appeals to images drawn from it could no longer legitimize the women's movement. References to women in a vocabulary drawn from civil rights and black power struggles disappeared. The once common reference to Betty Friedan as "the female Martin Luther King" was replaced by more descriptive adjectives such as author of the *Feminine Mystique*, or "mother of the movement."

The analogy between women and blacks, however, had opened up exploration of the condition of women. As a result, women saw they not only had been given a lower status in the public world, but they had been turned into mere objects in the home. Women were defined solely in terms of their relationships to others. They had no independent status.

The Act of Rejection

Out of this recognition, the Woman as Object metaphor appeared. This metaphor dominated the scene for a brief but active period of the movement. From the late 1960s until 1972 the metaphor provided the conceptual basis for the emergence of the radical feminists as a distinct group. Within the confines of the radicial feminist community, the Woman as Object became a basic tenet of feminist theory and was refined to focus on the role of women as Sex-Object.

Just as the descriptions of women in terms of civil rights images gradually faded away, the reporting of political activity in the *New York Times* took an important turn. Actions designed to reveal the objectification of women increased and became much more militant. During this period strategies and tactics expanded beyond the indictment of women's public roles. Voting, employment and legal restrictions remained targets for action, but the home and family came under attack. Women's political actions moved to challenge the private sphere as well. It was the extension of the metaphor into the *private* world that enabled women to reject the definition ascribed to them by society. The Miss America Pageant, marriage license bureaus, newspapers and a host of corporations and industries were assailed through law suits and public demonstrations.

Still having nothing to put in its place, women were no longer going to allow themselves to be characterized as passive objects defined by their relationships to men. Nor were they willing to accept as their sole purpose in life providing for the sexual pleasures of men. Consequently, the rejection of the prevailing definition of women also cast doubt upon the institutions of marriage and the family.

It was also during this period that radical feminist organizations were formed and began to flourish. The *New York Times* began to cover them as a separate group.

The focus of this chapter is to chart the development of the Woman as Object metaphor. The metaphor, given initial voice by the female radicals emerged most strongly within the radical feminist community and provided the basis for much of their thought and action throughout the decade of the 1970s.

Woman as Object

The 1960s culminated in a period of achievement for women. The *Times* welcomed the New Year of 1969 with a listing of the "firsts" won during the previous year. In Mississippi women were given the right to serve on juries; airlines were barred from dismissing stewardesses because of their age or marital status; want ads were no longer segregated into male and female jobs; the first women entered Yale (and the first man Vassar); Boy Scouts took in girl explorers, women took seats on the stock exchange and on the backs of race horses. In addition, women entered new areas of public life. The first African-American congresswoman in history was elected and two black women, Coretta Scott King of the Southern Christian Leadership Conference and Kathleen Cleaver of the Black Panthers, became the spokespersons for these groups. Among the "new left," women were now a "visible presence." So much so that the *Times*, ever attentive to women's fashions and manners, noted that the women of the left were now "wearing jeans" and using "four letter words" with ease.[1]

All of these "firsts" of course were the result of countless activities on the part of women across the country. During the next few years these activities became focused within a variety of organizations. By the beginning of the 1970s the movement had become conscious of itself as a force within the society and developed a deepening political and cultural perspective.

During this movement toward more solidified organizations and more forceful, united public action, the Woman as Nigger metaphor almost totally disappeared as either a justification for action or as a descriptive device. Its primary function was to be employed to attack the opposition to the movement. As such, it became a way to stress the "seriousness" of women's liberation.

Also vulnerable to the ridicule and scorn of its detractors, women were constantly confronted with the need to stress the importance of their movement. Only after years of struggle was the *Times* willing to comment that the movement "has finally achieved such widespread support that it was no longer being treated as a joke but as a serious revolution."[2] Part of the reason for the emergence of the serious status of the movement was the effectiveness with which women employed the comment: "You wouldn't say that if we were black men talking about racism!" Over and over again, some variation of this theme was employed during the early 1970s.

One of the best examples of this was an incident involving Betty Friedan. During a NOW conference, Friedan was invited to appear on a television talk show. The interview, unknown to Friedan, was designed to be a part of a fashion show. Furious at being tricked into appearing as a part of this setting, Friedan made an opening (and closing) statement the moment she could get on camera. She announced:

> I take outrageous exception to this program...I am considered the leader of a serious movement that concerns 58% of the population. To ask me to ap-

pear on a fashion show is like at the beginning of the civil rights movement to ask Martin Luther King to appear on a minstrel show.[3]

The fashion show, epitomizing the emerging metaphor of Woman as Object, cast women as passive objects to be decorated and admired. The show was soundly rejected in and of itself. The legitimacy garnered from the civil rights movement was no longer needed for this rejection. Rather, the civil rights contrast became a basis for attacking the inability of the interviewer to recognize the inappropriateness of the setting.

The initial probing of what it means to be a woman made possible by the earlier analogy was no longer able to provide direction or unity to the movement. As Black nationalism mounted in the late 1960s and as racial tensions increased throughout the country, the metaphor lost its power.

Women began to unite behind a forceful rejection of the identity society had defined for them. Unable to offer a counter definition, women were at least clear about what they were *not*. It was through this act of rejection that women first explored the prevailing notions of women and then countered them. Strongly attacking the dehumanizing aspects of the existing social definition, the metaphor Woman as Object emerged to thrust the movement toward a deeper definition of femaleness.

Again the female radicals provided the initial vocabulary to conceptualize Woman as Object. Drawing on the concepts of ownership and power, they realized that describing women in terms of the political categories of "second class citizenship" and "exploitation" were not enough. They discovered that women had no definition as autonomous beings. Rather, women were totally defined in terms of their relationships to others. Meridith Tax offers an example of this metaphor when she comments:

...for a woman is either an object (turned to stone), belonging to some man and getting her money, status, friends and very identity from her association with him—or else she is nowhere, disappeared, teetering on the edge of a void with no work to do and no felt identity at all..girls are taught to see themselves as objects rather than as subjects.[4]

Women began to argue that they had been "defined by those other than ourselves" and had been ascribed to possess qualities that "are not in our interest." As a result, they pledged that they must now "cease to be defined by men" and to begin to "define ourselves" by unearthing the "missing pieces of history" and by discovering our "lost traditions." Women were no longer going to be content with a room of their own, they were "out to discover a world of their own."[5]

Radical Feminists on the Rise

The female radicals, having contributed to the theoretical statement of the problem and the actual articulation of the metaphor, did not use it to provide the impetus for united public action. This task was left to the emerging group of women calling themselves radical feminists. The radical feminists embraced the metaphor Woman as Object. They gave it its life and depth. It became central to their developing theories of "feminism" and to the kind of actions and strategies they advocated.

Radical feminists, many of whom had been schooled in the movement of the "new left," recognized the objectification of women took a particular form in American society—sex. Women were not only treated as passive objects, they were turned into sex objects for the pleasure of men.

These radical feminists were young, bright, well

educated and often near celebrity status. As a result they were skilled in dealing with the media. They were often imaginative in their efforts to create public demonstrations to dramatize their points. Most notable among these early feminists were such women as Josephine Duke and Robin Morgan. Duke, a member of one of the most politically and socially prominent families in the country, intrigued the media with her boldness. Her dress, language and verbal and physical assaults on authority made her a particularly interesting "story." And Robin Morgan, described as a "young, radical poet," had gained the affection of the nation during her portrayal of Dagmar in the television series "I Remember Mama." The thought of Dagmar as a women's "libber" was more than the media could resist.

As members of Women's Liberation, a New York-based group of about 150 radical-left women, they attracted the attention of the *Times* and the whole nation by staging a protest demonstration before the Miss America Pageant. Here the Woman as Object metaphor was firmly established and thrust into national prominence. The radical feminists argued that the Miss America Pageant epitomized the objectification of women. They argued that the pageant turned women into "degrading, mindless, boob-girlie" symbols. Staging guerilla theater, crowning a sheep and setting up trash cans for women to disgard the "symbols of their oppression—bras, eye lashes, playboy magazines and steno pads," the demonstration shocked Americans. Signs read:

Miss America Sells It
The Living Bra—the Dead Soldier
Girls Crowned—Boys Killed

The image of demure graduate students carrying these signs was more than even a nation that had become somewhat used to demonstrations and public satire could take.[6]

The Women's Liberation Organization however was concerned with more than shocking Americans. They had developed a position paper to document the political content of their goals. These goals went far beyond simply attacking the image of women as sex objects. They explained the Miss America Pageant was deliberately chosen because it represented a larger evil. The pageant had been traditionally "lily white." The winner was given a tour of Viet Nam and hence turned into a "murder mascot." And the whole purpose behind the event was to promote products and increase corporate profits. The feminists stated:

Where else could one find such perfect combination of American values: Racism, militarism and capitalism—all packaged in one ideal symbol: A woman.[7]

For the radical feminists, the role of women as objects led to an indictment of the larger social, political and economic system. Women were seen as being defined as consumers, reduced to victims of a technology they had been brainwashed to believe benefited them and turned into commodities. Thus, the metaphor shapes the indictment of the larger system:

...the uniquely visible conditions of women as primarily sexual creatures, as decorative, tempting, passive pleasure giving objects, exposes the broader framework of social coercion...Our strategy is not for equal jobs but meaningful, creative activity. It is not to share the power but to abolish commodity tyranny, not for an equal sex role but to end the objectification and exploitation.[8]

The radical feminists then began to develop both a new theory of political action and new organizations in which to practice this action. For despite the growing numbers of women in "new left" politics, with fully 30% of those arrested during the Columbia uprisings being women, radical feminists were no longer willing to fight with the male chauvinists within the "movement." As Robin Morgan so clearly stated, from their perspective: "A lot of movement women might just as well have gone to Scarsdale."[9] And NOW, with it reformist emphasis on equality and sharing the way things were was clearly not adequate.

The Offended Offense

The Women's Liberation activity at the Miss America Pageant did not go without notice or without attack. Their larger political goals were somewhat obscured by the very success of their indictment of the objectification of women. Most Americans were horrified at the intensity of the ridicule directed at such a sacred symbol of American womanhood. Nonetheless establishment than columnist Harriet Van Horne was provoked to publicly admonish the group for its "childish" behavior. Letters to the *Times* suggested "good spankings" for the women.[10] Van Horne went so far as to suggest that this kind of public behavior could only be the result of women who had been "exposed to the wrong man." She proudly proclaimed to speak for most women saying we would rather "be somebody's girl than nobody's cum laude."[11]

Yet despite the vehemence of her attack, Van Horne was forced to admit that the radical feminists had "some truth in the mindless boob" image. A truth not compelling enough to shape up Ms. Van Horne, to be sure, but it clearly fueled the "fury" and "anger" that the radical feminists had helped to unleash.

The Attack on Marriage

It was precisely the truth in this metaphor that enabled the radical feminists, female radicals and liberal feminists to maintain some cohesion and direction.

A host of organizations and manifestos sprang up. Even the usually sedate coverage of the Food, Fashion, Family and Furnishings section of the *Times* was forced to record the growing political activity fostered by this metaphor. For example, a traditional bridal fair held in Madison Square Garden to introduce the new line of fashions became of special interest when picketed by WITCH. WITCH, or Women's International Terrorist Conspiracy from Hell, modeled itself after the Yippies. Complete with black hats and brooms they staged an "unwedding ceremony," singing "here come the slaves, off to their graves." In a show of fun and greeted by surprisingly tolerant good humor, WITCH brought the house to its feet by unleashing 100 white mice in the stadium.[12]

These public demonstrations by the radical feminists coincided with rapid changes in the lives of the "average" woman. The *Times* attempted to document the "new breed of middle-class woman."

Marilyn Bender begins by noting:

> For a decade, she's been scrutinized and criticized,
> pressurized and radicalized. Her malaise has been
> called "the woman thing," the "emptiness thing"
> and the "feminine mystique," the title of a book
> by Betty Freidan in 1963 that goaded women to
> fly out of their nests and into a career or a cause.

And women had taken to the flight. As Jessie Bernard went on to state in the article:

In the midst of rebellion (youthful and sexual) and assorted crises of city and race, the Super-mother, the Super-consumer and the Lady Bountiful are out of style. The American women may have gained legal rights...but she has lost the option to stay home.[13]

Having succeeded in establishing that the home was not enough for women, radical feminists began a full scale attack on marriage. Here the blending of the Woman as Nigger and Woman as Object combine on a theoretical level. Radical feminists began to conceptualize marriage as a form of slavery. This fused metaphor became a theoretical tenet of the radical feminists and the basis of much of their ongoing political activity. For example, the Feminist Organization became a regular presence in front of the New York City marriage license bureau. At one point they targeted a ceremony honoring, of all people, Tony Bennet. Five women of the Feminist Organization stormed into the marriage license bureau during the event, condemning marriage as a system "in which women are being illegally made sex slaves in the unholy state of matrimony.[14] Ti-Grace Atkinson, the spokesperson of the group and one of its leading theoreticians drew upon the fused metaphor as the basis for her theoretical work. While the whole event was treated in a somewhat lighthearted vein by the *Times*, the implications of this direct assault on marriage were not lost on the liberal feminists or the larger society.

The Breakdown of the Metaphor

NOW found itself increasingly uneasy with the radical agenda being put forward. The equation of marriage with slavery was uncomfortable. The larger indictment of society was threatening, especially when so much of NOW's own efforts were to be included into the very system the radical feminists were attacking. And NOW was concerned that many of the tactics of the more radical groups would only alienate much needed support. Consequently NOW moved ahead to try and develop some middle ground. They decided to call a Congress to Unite Women. With much persuasion, the Congress succeeded in bringing together members of NOW with Women's Liberation and a host of radical feminist groups. The Congress made no serious efforts at ideological or theoretical unity. Instead they emphasized action through a series of proposals that all women agreed upon: 24 hour day care, women's study programs in colleges and universities, equality of employment, the right to an abortion and an equal rights amendment. The program was announced as a unified plan. Demonstrating a commitment of the avoidance of male leadership styles, it was agreed by all members of the Congress to have the program presented to the press by a young woman who was to remain anonymous.[15] In many ways this simple agenda became a basic outline of areas for action by women for the next few years.

Yet the show of unity and the generally agreed upon direction of the movement were covering over some growing divisions. Feminist theory was evolving rapidly. Radical feminists took over the theoretical leadership of the movement and generated a host of new concepts and ideas. Growing out of the fused metaphor Woman as Nigger and Woman as Object, radical feminists advanced ideas demonstrating how women had been defined *out* of participation in political life. History was revised and reconceptualized as being divided along sex-lines. The sex-struggle replaced the class struggle as patriarchy became the prevailing indictment of the "system." For the first time MAN was identified as the enemy. All those aspects of private life that had been important to women were openly attacked. The home and family were cast as the source of oppression. Issues of reform and revolution opened a host of antagonisms. The very nature of the public demonstrations became controversial.

At the same time as these antagonisms were growing, the importance of women's experiences as the source of all theory and ideas was evolving within the radical feminist community. The Woman as Object metaphor had given radical feminists a way to begin to conceptualize women's experience in a new way. The energy and power that the metaphor unleashed became the basis for initiating the most successful strategy of the movement, the consciousness-raising groups. It was in the course of these groups that an emphasis was placed on the validity of personal experience. Sharing this experience became an important goal. As one woman explained:

> No matter which road we follow, we all have two things to do: to liberate ourselves and to liberate each other. We can't do one without the other and we can't do either unless we do both.[16]

Thus the desire to maintain unity again emerges. Knowing that "our strength as individuals is directly proportional to our strength as a group" women began through the consciousness-raising groups to:

> ...support each other through shared experiences with compassion and sympathy. We will find liberation only through unity.[17]

It was in the confines of these groups that the disunity was again submerged.

NOTES

1. Judy Klemesrud, "1968: For Women It Was a Year Marked by Firsts," *New York Times*, 1 January 1969, p. 25.

2. Ibid., p. 25.

3. *New York Times*, 23 March 1970.

4. Ann Koedt, Ellen Levin and Anita Rapone, *Radical Feminism* (New York: Quadrangle, 1973), p. 31.

5. Anne Gottlieb, "Female Human Beings," *New York Times*, 17 February 1971, p. 26.

6. Peter Babcox, "Meet the Women of the Revolution, 1969," *New York Times*, 9 February 1969, p. 34.

7. Ibid., p. 34.

8. Ibid., p. 85.

9. Ibid., p. 88.

10. "Letters," *New York Times*, 2 March 1969, VI, p. 6.

11. Babcox, p. 85.

12. Judy Klemesrud, "It Was A Special Show and the Audience Was Special, Too," *New York Times*, 17 February 1969, p. 29.

13. Marilyn Bender, "A New Breed of Middle-Class Women Emerging," *New York Times*, 17 March 1969, p. 34.

14. Alfred S. Clark, "Five Women Protest the 'Slavery' of Marriage," *New York Times*, 24 September 1969, p. 93.

15. Linda Greenhouse, "Women's Group Pressuring Reforms," *New York Times*, 25 November 1969, p. 51.

16. "A Woman's Place Is in the Oven," *New York Times*, 10 October 1971, II, p. 11.

17. Gottlieb.

CHAPTER V
The Woman as Persona

The energy and power unleashed by the Woman as Object metaphor began to trouble many women in the movement. The raucous demonstrations, the "outlandish" dress and the open disdain for marriage and the family expressed by many of the new radical feminists made both the female radicals and the liberal feminists uncomfortable. To the female radicals, the emphasis on patriarchy and the concept of sex as a class diverted attention away from the real enemy, capitalism. And to the liberal feminists, anxious to become a part of capitalism, the outrageous behavior of the female radicals and the attack on the family made the movement seem alien and vulnerable to attack. Thus while the Woman as Object maintained a secure place within radical feminist theory, it quickly became incapable of providing unity. Almost as soon as women had vividly expressed their collective NO! to the existing definition of womanhood, the metaphor began to wane.

By 1970 radical feminists, having denounced the societal definition of woman, began to search for a new positive identity. They realized that not only women, but seemingly the whole world had been defined by men. With this in mind, they argued that everything had to be reconceptualized to reflect a woman's point of view. The Woman as Persona began as the desire to uncover the world of women, their lives, hopes, and dreams. Under this metaphor, the descriptive adjectives used by the *Times* took a dramatic shift. The passive, pathetic object of wife and mother was gone. In her place emerged the creative, imaginative and energetic woman of the early 1970s.

This creative energy resulted in an outpouring of books, articles and pamphlets on virtually every aspect of women's experience from childbirth to life in the executive suite or life underground. Ten major books appeared in 1970 causing the *New York Times* to devote separate articles to the emergence of women in literature.

Beginning with the Women's Strike for Equality in 1970, the metaphor gradually developed as women began to explore their own experience as independent beings. It was expressed most clearly in the strategy that became the hallmark of the movement—consciousness-raising. This marked a clear shift from the earlier strategies as massive public demonstrations became less important. Small groups became the life of the movement as hundreds of thousands of women began to gather together to discuss their lives and ideas. These discussions brought a new challenge and vitality to what had traditionally been defined as political activity. In addition, they brought a growing awareness of not only the joy of being a woman, but they began to uncover some of the pain and anguish. Thus through the early 1970s women began to define for themselves who they were. Their own experience became their guide. This chapter explores the development of that process.

The Personal Is Political

Faced with growing divisions and increasingly rigid and contradictory ideologies, the movement entered a crisis in 1970. Unable to achieve ideological coherence, let alone unity, the movement simply abandoned the drive for an agreed upon ideology. The anti-intellectualism of the "new left" was taken on by women with a vengeance. Women from Ti-Grace Atkinson to Betty Friedan claimed that women's personal experience was to be the measure of all things.

This emphasis on personal experience further validated the consciousness-raising groups. Women began to recognize that much of their lives, ignored for centuries, was in fact important. Washing dishes, being a waitress, having and raising children, all activities ignored or devalued by our society, were reasserted as positive and essential human actions. Woman as a state of "being" became the most salient aspect of the movement.

For the first time, the adjectives appearing in the *Times* applied to women began to change. No longer compared to hot house plants or troubled, discontented and emotional shriekers, women became: creative, energetic, imaginative, independent. The decade of the 1970's was proclaimed as "a great time to be a woman."[1]

Filled with the celebration of being female, there was an outpouring of intellectual activity, especially among the radical feminists. In fact, 10 books were slated for publication in 1970. The *Times* book review section, used to doing one or two articles a year on books pertaining to women, developed a separate article discussing the forthcoming publications. On the list were: Juliet Mitchell's, *The Longest Revolution*; Gornic and Moran's *Fifty One Percent: the Case for Women's Liberation*, Kate Millet's *Sexual Politics*, Firestone's *Dialectics of Sex*, Turner's *The Women's Liberation Movement* and Toni Cade's anthology of black women. Morgan was editing *The Hand that Cradles the Rock*, only

86

to be forced to change the title to *Sisterhood Is Powerful*.[2]

Of all of these works, *Sexual Politics* by Kate Millet was greeted with the most critical acclaim. The *Times* reviewer compared her to De Beauvoir and Lessing. And the book was thought to exemplify the best of the movement, the blend of intellect and emotion that women hoped to bring to public life.[3]

All of this intellectual activity helped to advance and clarify the basic principles of radical feminist theory: patriarchy, the sexual division of labor, sex as a class, man as the enemy and the need for a radical transformation of society.

However, the core of radical feminist theory was the belief in the sisterhood of women and the importance of personal experience. The essence of this philosophy was articulated by Robin Morgan in the introduction to *Sisterhood Is Powerful*:

> The only hope of a new feminist movement is some kind of only now barely emerging politics of *revolutionary feminism*, which some people are trying to explore in this anthology.
>
> That politics comes from what has been called "rap sessions," "bitch sessions," or "consciousness-raising" which the small groups of radical women began to form around 1966-67.[4]

Thus as the very sharpness of the emerging radical feminist theory created distinctions within the movement, the emphasis on sisterhood and personal experience provided a basis for unity. It was not the analysis of politics and power which took hold with such force. Rather, the Woman as Persona emerged with the implied strategy of consciousness-raising groups. Based on the ideological premise that experience was the basis of theory and a source of strength, literally hundreds of thousands of consciousness-raising groups were established. Questions to aid the sessions as well as suggestions for the format were first circulated by hand on mimeograph sheets, then printed in *Sisterhood* and within articles in the *Times*. These guidelines became a basis around which women could meet together to explore their lives. They were simple aids to discussion, intending to encourage women to speak and to look at their own experience. Typical of the questions:

> Discuss your relationship with men. Have you noticed any recurring patterns?
>
> Have you ever felt that men pressured you into sexual relationships?
>
> Have you ever lied about orgasm?
>
> Discuss your relationship to other women. Did you compete?
>
> Growing up as a girl were you treated differently from your brother?
>
> What would you most like to do in life? What stopped you?[5]

The power of these discussions to radicalize women was noted across the country. Susan Brownmiller, in a summary article in March of 1970 discusses the pervasiveness of women's liberation:

> Women's liberation is hot stuff this season, in media terms, and no wonder. In the short space of two years, the new feminism has taken hold and rooted in territory that at first glance appears an unlikely breeding ground for revolutionary ideas:

among urban, white, college educated middle class
women generally considered to be a rather privileged lot by those thought to know their politics,
or know their women.[6]

During this period, issues of race and class were thought
to be submerged under the banner of sisterhood. And
sisterhood, the bond of personal experience as women,
became the driving force of the movement.

Women began to characterize themselves as the "only
oppressed group who have lived divided from one another
and in intimacy with their masters in a chronic state of
bribery and intimidation." Above all else, then, was the need
"to get ourselves together," to "build stable deeply ground-
ed female world" and to "divest ourselves from all
preconceptions and walk into the unknown."[7]

All women, regardless of what they thought, or didn't
think, regardless of race, or class were united by the deeper
level of their common experience as women. The depth of
this belief is seen in the radical feminist conception of the
Movement:

This is not a movement one joins. There are no rigid
structures of membership cards. The Women's
Liberation Movement exists where three or four
friends or neighbors decide to meet regularly over
coffee and talk about their personal lives. It also
exists in the cells of women's jails, in the welfare
lines, in the supermarket, the factory, the convent,
the farm, the maternity ward, the streetcorner, the
old ladies' home, the kitchen, the steno pool, the
bed. It exists in your mind, and in the political and
personal insights that you can contribute to change
and shape and help its growth. It's frightening. It
is very exhilarating. It is creating history, or rather,
herstory.

And anyway, you cannot escape it.[8]

And in truth, this sense of sisterhood did enable the radical feminists to transcend many of their own ideological positions to accept, reach out and be open to other women. Perhaps no where is the power of the Woman as Persona more powerfully demonstrated than in Robin Morgan's response to the Watergate women. Morgan as a radical, a feminist, an ardent political and social activist, was about as far to the opposite end of the political spectrum from Pat Nixon as anyone could get. Yet during the painful national experience of Watergate, it was Morgan who was able to transcend her political position to capture with extraordinary sympathy and gentleness the pain of Pat Nixon as she sat and silently watched the destruction of her husband and herself.[9]

During this period the unity of women was the paramount concern. Anything anyone wanted to say was fine. Women were to support one another, not disagree or challenge. There is no doubt that this period succeeded in creating an atmosphere in which women found the courage to speak. In addition it created a new texture to the understanding of the daily experience of women as valuable and worthwhile.

The phrase "the personal is political" became a rallying cry serving to provide the theoretical justification for the discussion and discovery of day to day life. This concept became a powerful weapon within the ranks of radical/progressive women as well for it became a way to confront, on *theoretical* grounds, many of the concepts of politics advanced by men. In particular, the idea that political and personal life were somehow separated, with political life being a superior activity, was attacked.

Men who for years had been able to "avoid" or scorn the life of family and household, suddenly found their political orientation being challenged because of their personal practices. Lenin, the revolutionary figure revered by many for his single-minded approach to revolution, was "revised" to be ridiculed and condemned for his treatment of his wife. Personal, private life burst forward to challenge traditional notions of "correct" political ideas and practices. This theoretical insight meant that "hypocrisy" would no longer be tolerated. Political activity had to become embodied in the practice of daily life. No more talking about new human relationships and continuing to live in a household dominated by male chauvinism. No more concern for the environment and tossing cigarettes on the ground. In short, the concept of "the personal is political" demanded that political people (especially men) literally get their houses and themselves in order.[10]

This reshaping of the boundary between politics and personal life had the positive effect of demanding a greater congruence between what people said and what they did. It also expanded the narrow confines of what had been considered political action to make what people did in their daily lives have greater meaning.

At the same time, the Woman as Persona contained within it many contradictory elements. In the effort to create a supportive environment, serious criticism and evaluation of ideas were simply not tolerated. Intellectual fuzziness became the price of unity.

And while infusing politics with a new energy and vigor by drawing on personal experience, the relationship of women to political analysis and power became more and more obscured under the weight of personal experience and unity. The personal became the sum-total of political experience. Nowhere is this more clearly demonstrated than in the evolution of the work of Kate Millet during this period.

It was Millet whose insight and intellect had so brilliantly drawn out the political basis of sexual oppression and who had most clearly articulated the relationship between sexuality and power. Yet in her second book, *Flying*, and subsequent writing in *Ms.*, Millet shifted her focus away from the discussion of political concepts. Rather she chose to almost denegrate her own political exploration and to document instead the personal and painful trauma she was experiencing as a woman and as a lesbian who had become one of the most visible representatives of the "movement."[11]

Some years later, Millet exemplified the metaphor in a defense of *Flying*, arguing that it was the very intensity of her personal revelations which made it objectionable. She contrasted it with the careful political analysis of *Sexual Politics*:

> All that *Sexual Politics* has come to stand for... respect, ability, erudition, objective and theoretical impersonality...all this is overturned and for the rigid minded...even "betrayed" by the absolute *personality* of *Flying*. The trouble with *Flying* is simple: its the personhood; not the sweeping generalities of patriarchal society but the private and unique case.[12]

As a result of the emphasis on personal experience, with political analysis restricted,in a curious way the private sphere was opened up to be stripped of its most central humanizing elements. The open attack on marriage and the family persisted. Buttressed by the concept of Woman as Sex Object and legitimized by the belief that all personal/private areas of life were open to political scrutiny and action, radical feminists directed more and more of their political activity away from the institutions of politics and power in the public world and more toward those that circumscribed women's private lives. Thus the inherent tension between public and private spheres of human activity had been expanded and then quickly blurred as any real distinctions between the two spheres were lost.

Women's Strike for Equality:

Under the banner of unity NOW began its most daring campaign. Betty Friedan, retiring as president of NOW, used the occasion of her retirement speech to announce the decision (unknown to just about everyone in NOW) that August 26th, 1970 would be a day for a general strike by women to honor the 50th anniversary of the women's right to vote.[13]

The decision to go ahead with the strike was a difficult one for NOW. But since the remark by Friedan had been picked up by the press, the executive committee thought they had no real choice but to work for it. As in the previous Congress to Unite Women, NOW took steps to draw in the radical feminists, radical lesbians and female radicals. While this created an uneasy alliance on ideological grounds, Friedan and NOW took the position that as long as everyone was working for the same goals, everyone could just "do their own thing."[14]

And this is precisely what women did. Throughout the spring and summer, the movement around consciousness-raising continued to grow. The *Times* noted that it had even reached the peaceful, affluent suburbs surrounding New York City. They commented:

> It came quietly, almost timidly—a few friends meeting in an afternoon to share ideas. But within 2 months membership in the Croton Women's Liberation Organization was 50.[15]

This quiet movement was happening all across the country. But "quiet" wasn't the only way women were moving. Radical feminists continued to expand their efforts at reconceptualizing women in the home. Ti-Grace Atkinson, in a speech before the National Council of Christians and Jews, called upon Women's Liberation to see that the pro-

stitutes were the "most courageous leaders of the revolution." She argued that prostitutes were the only "honest
women left in America" because they "charge for it rather
than submit to men."[16]

The offices of the Ladies Home Journal became the
target of a sit-in by women demanding an issue devoted to
liberation and an end to the portrayal of women as mindless
commodities. Women took over abandoned buildings, setting up women's centers and headquarters for women only.
And they got themselves arrested and abused in their efforts to fend off eviction by the police.[17]

The energy and activity generated by these events
touched the radical community as SDS confronted male
chauvinism in its convention and decided that personal life
must now be integrated with revolutionary concerns.[18]

As August drew closer, all these diverse activities began
to focus on the nationwide protest. Women were reported
to be planning everything from baby-ins to marches with
the goal of bringing about equal employment opportunities
for women, free abortions and childcare.

Avoiding ideological questions, the movement at this
point focused almost totally on tactics and strategies.
Freedom trash cans were proposed to line the parade route.
Women made plans to liberate the Statue of Liberty. Tot-
ins were staged and a new symbol of the movement made
its appearance. Evoking images of black power, women
adopted the clenched fist inside the biological symbol for
women.[19]

"Don't Iron while the Strike Is Hot"

On August 26 over 10,000 women marched down Fifth
Avenue. Finally after a decade of coverage, the movement
hit the front page of the *Times*. Everyone was amazed at
the depth of the participation by women not only in New

York but in towns across the country.[20] But the coverage still managed to keep everything from being "too serious." The follow-up articles on the back pages of the paper proclaimed: "Leading Feminist Puts Hairdo before Strike." Rather than a discussion of the reasons for the march, Friedan's hair appointment dominated the story.[21] In addition the *Times* attempted to minimize the impact of the march by noting that "For Most Women Strike Day was Just a Topic of Conversation."[22]

Yet the women involved in the strike knew it represented a plateau in the movement. Kate Millet commented:

> We have marched curb to curb, we tonight became
> the great new force in politics for social change in
> the 1970s.[23]

More than any other comment, this illustrates the new image of women. The strike put to rest the need to compare women to something else. It gave women a sense of their own power, in their own right. Having been defined as passive objects, women had not only rejected the definition, but they had gained the courage from one another to begin the long crusade to explore just exactly who they were.

Again, the Opposition

The strike and all of the surrounding activity provoked reactions. The women's movement was no longer laughed at or ridiculed. Rather the opposition began to seriously attack the members. The movement was called a "lesbian plot" (which in 1970 was about as strong a method of discrediting the movement as calling it a communist plot). It was described as being comprised of nothing but a "group of frustrated old maids who needed a good man." And small groups began to spring up to counter the feminist organizations. The *Times* took care in reporting these. For example, the *Times* noted the Pussy Cat League being formed with the slogan "purr baby purr."[24]

These organizations were coupled with the advent of a public spokeswoman for the "silent majority" who argued that for most Americans (outside of the few New York radicals) the "woman's place was still in the home." Helen Andeline, a 50 year old housewife from Santa Barbara began a national promotion tour of her book, *Fascinating Womanhood*. Appearing across the country on talk shows and interviews, Ms. Andeline took great care to create a "feminine presence." She began to advocate a Womanhood Day to celebrate "our feminity."[25]

Nor was this opposition confined within the ranks of the silent majority or the dedicated male-chauvinists. Dr. Spock, whose advice had helped to shape the generation of women now protesting, raised the question, "But why can't a woman be less like a man?" And he pondered, ever concerned for children, "Who will take care of children as more women go to college?"[26]

The Breakdown

As the enthusiasm for the women's strike began to fade, differences again began to surface. First, NOW became more and more sensitive to the charge of "lesbianism." On the one hand women wanted to deny the participation of lesbians in the movement. On the other hand, many lesbians and other women were demanding that their "sisters" be given greater respect and appreciation. Thus the issue of homosexuality became a tremendous source of controversy. The abortion issue also became clearly identified with the movement, beginning to lay the basis for opposition to the movement among the emerging right-to-life groups.

Class and race differences again emerged. Especially as "men" became characterized as the enemy, many working class, black and minority women felt there was no place for them in the movement. And certainly no place for them as long as they valued their family lives and community ties. The alienation felt by black women is expressed in Nikki Giovanni's assessment of the movement:

> Women's liberation is basically a family quarrel between white women and white men. And on general principles it's not good to get involved in family disputes. Outsiders always get shafted when the dust settles.[27]

The issue of reform versus revolution also continued to plague the movement. It became especially serious as NOW devoted more of its energies to equipping women to become "equal partners" in the capitalist system and to aiming its activity in the legislative realm. Over the next period NOW saw its role as helping to defeat the Carswell nomination for the Supreme Court. It actively pursued alliances with business and industry.[28]

Both the tensions and the energy of this period were reflected in the founding of *Ms.* Magazine. *Ms.* was self-consciously pro-feminist. It provided a strong liberal voice for both reform and revolution. Avidly pro-abortion it nonetheless took an affirmative stance on issues involving family life. As a popular magazine, it was determined to have a broad popular appeal.

Thus during the late 1960s and early 1970s there are the first steps toward creating an independent female identity. Having rejected the definitions provided by the male dominated society women began to seek a new understanding of themselves. Yet this new understanding found its roots in the private, personal world, not in an analysis of the political relationships inherent in the public sphere.

Women's personal, day to day lives were explored and discussed. And in the process, the diversity of ideas, experiences and beliefs that were inherent in women could no longer be easily set aside.

And more troubling, as the reality of women's lives became clear, it turned out that she wasn't a goddess after all. The "pedestal" and "gilded cage" were discovered to be surrounded by shadows of violence and fear.

NOTES

1. Gottlieb.

2. Marilyn Bender, "Books to Liberate Women," *New York Times,* 8 March 1970, VII, p. 10.

3. Christopher Lehmann-Haupt, "He and She," *New York Times,* 5 August 1970, p. 33.

4. Robin Morgan, *Sisterhood Is Powerful,* p. xxiii.

5. Susan Brownmiller, " 'Sisterhood is Powerful': A Member of the Women's Liberation Movement Explains What It's All About," *New York Times,* 15 March 1970, VI, p. 27.

6. Ibid., p. 27.

7. Gottlieb.

8. Morgan, Sisterhood, p. xxxvi.

9. Robin Morgan, "On Watergate Women," *Ms.,* April 1974.

10. Morgan, *Sisterhood,* pp. xx-xxix.

11. Kate Millet, "Pain of Public Sorting," *Ms.,* June 1974, p. 76-79.

12. Kate Millet, "Forum-Shame Millet," *Ms.,* January 1975. p. 27

13. Dierdra Carmody, "General Strike by Women Urged to Mark 2974 Amendment," *New York Times,* 21 March 1970, p. 21.

14. Judy Klemesrud, "A Herstory-Making Event," *New York Times,* 23 August 1970, VI, p. 6.

15. Linda Greenhouse, "Feminist Efforts Grow in Croton," *New York Times,* 5 April 1970, p. 53.

16. Lacey Fosburg, "Women's Liberation Hails the Prostitutes," *New York Times,* 29 May 1970, p. 30.

17. Marilyn Bender, "Women's Lib Headquarters," *New York Times,* 1 July 1970. p. 54, and "Unused City Building Seized by 20

Feminists," *New York Times*, 2 January 1971, p. 13.

18. Will Lissner, "New Left Groups in Session Here," *New York Times*, 19 July 1970, p. 33.

19. Klemesrud, "A Herstory."

20. Linda Charlton, "Women March Down Fifth in Equality Day," *New York Times*, 27 August 1970, p. 1.

21. "Leading Feminist Puts Hairdo Before Strike," *New York Times*, 27 August 1970, p. 30.

22. Craig Lichtenstein, "For Most Women Strike Day Was Just a Topic of Conversation," *New York Times*, 27 August 1970, p. 30.

23. Linda Charlton, "The Feminist Protest," *New York Times*, 28 August 1970, p. 20.

24. Judy Klemesrud, "It was a Great Day for Women on the March," *New York Times*, 30 August 1970, IV, p. 4.

25. Joan Cook, "She Takes a Stand Against Liberation," *New York Times*, 28 September 1970, p. 50.

26. Israel Shenker, "Spock Still Cares About Babies, Wishes More Women Did," *New York Times*, 28 January 1970, p. 38.

27. *New York Times*, 22 August 1971, VI, p. 14.

28. "Carswell Called Foe of Women's Rights," *New York Times*, 30 January 1970, p. 20.

CHAPTER VI

Woman as Victim: Consummation

During the Woman as Persona metaphor, women became painfully aware that much of their existence was surrounded by brutality. The rich diversity of the female experience began to take on a sordid dimension. By the mid-1970s the dehumanization of pornography, the reality of rape and domestic violence and the ugliness of illegal abortions all became central concerns of the movement. Each of these issues was chronicled in the *New York Times*. *Ms.* became a forum for their in-depth exploration. The comforting talk of consciousness-raising gave way to the strident organizing of crisis centers, aggressive self-help networks and highly charged campaigns on abortion and pornography. Women had come to a clear definition of who they were. They were victims. But they were not the passive, compliant Objects of years before. They were victims who had begun to fight back. Women recognized their own victimage and the necessity of taking decisive actions to counter it.

The struggle for the ERA also emerged during this period and was documented in the *Times* coverage. Beginning with the defeat of the ERA in New York, more and more of the efforts of the movement were channeled into passage of the amendment. To women and to their foes, the ERA became the symbolic battleground of a national referendum on the role of women.

In the course of these struggles totally new concepts were put forward. Sexuality was separated from violence and erotica from pornography. At the same time, both the struggle for the ERA, for abortion and for laws and programs to assist women began to pull the movement toward electoral politics. Grant writing and lobbying became important actions. Step by step women tied themselves to government grants, friendly politicians and traditional political campaigns. More and more coverage in the *New York Times* began to focus on women within the electoral process. As a result, they ceased to be "outsiders." They became a clearly defined interest group operating within the context of traditional politics. In essence, the women's movement ceased to challenge the fundamental direction of American society. It became a part of it.

This chapter details the development of the Woman as Victim and begins to explore the subtle shift into the electoral world.

Divisions Resurface

The early 1970s saw women moving into virtually every sphere of American life from which they had been traditionally excluded. College campuses across the nation began courses in women's studies exploring the history and present condition of women. While attacked sometimes as a "slightly absurd idea" or "a radical innovation," the classes provided a forum for addressing the "omission and distortions of traditional education."[1] Women, now over 40% of the workforce, achieved the status of no longer being "dilet- tantes."[2] The very language came under attack. Words like policemen, firemen and chairmen were repudiated for not reflecting reality. On a deeper level, the structure of English itself was called into question as women began a full scale assault on the language as the "most positive and express- ly masculine of languages." They argued that women were forced to see themselves through "male mirrors which dis- tort and insult them."[3]

The adjectives employed by the *Times* took another dramatic shift. Active, intelligent and creative were augmented by a series of words indicating the growing anger of women. "Speaking angrily" and "harshly," "overturn- ing laws," being "resentful" and "filled with wrath" began to be common descriptions of the mood of women as they moved full steam into the 1970s.[4]

As the decade unfolded, much of the anger and hostili- ty unleashed was not all directed at men or the system. For the first time, open splits in the movement were reported in the *Times*. The richness of personal experience uncovered by the exploration of women's lives in consciousness-raising groups and in countless articles and papers revealed more real diversity and differences than even the most enthusi- astic women had thought possible. Racial differences were brought into focus as black women started to hold meetings and discuss their concerns. These concerns were of course markedly different from those of the white middle-class women who dominated NOW and radical feminist groups. Black women pointed out that rather than being anti-male, they were concerned with how to help "junkie husbands." Rather than wanting an equal spot in the executive offices, they emphasized the conditions of domestic workers, still the primary source of employment for black women. Welfare reform and prison reform were of vital concern.[5]

The 1972 election reflected the disaffection of many

women with "the movement." In analyzing the returns in which the majority of women did not vote for feminist issues or candidates, Gloria Steinem was forced to admit that the "movement hasn't reached the women who need it most."[6] Working class women, women outside of the narrow, college-educated professional circle, still looked upon the movement as having little to do with them or their own lives.

As troubling as the inability of the movement to reach beyond a narrow base was the emergence of deep divisions within the movement itself. Older women began to feel rejected and scorned by the younger members. While radical feminist leaders such as Ti-Grace Atkinson acknowledged that "older women are the garbage of society," the reality of the interaction between older and younger women led to the formation of OWL (Older Women's Liberation) as a way to deal with the tensions that arose. Older women struck out on their own.

All of these divisions were compounded by the solidifying of ideological positions among the various women's organizations. Increased splintering, distrust and open fighting began. By the summer of 1972 Friedan publicly admitted that "deep ideological differences" were "tearing apart the movement." The intensity of these differences can be seen in her attack on the founding of *Ms.* Magazine.

Ms. began as an idea for a simple newsletter to "connect" women and keep them informed of activities and ideas in the movement. But as the few radical feminists began to meet and talk about how the newsletter should look, who it should reach and what purpose it could serve, the concept of a popular magazine came up. Explaining this in their first regularly scheduled edition, *Ms.* reported that the:

> ...idea of a full fledged national magazine came up;
> a publication created and controlled by women that
> could be as serious, outrageous, satisfying, sad,
> funky, intimate, global, compassionate and full of

change as women's lives really are.[7]

Yet this rather innocent and playful idea was not greeted with universal glee. Betty Friedan, by now called the "mother superior of the movement," openly attacked Gloria Steinem and the other editors. She said they were attempting to "rip off" the movement by moving to a "commercial operation." While later saying she had been misquoted, the fight was on.[8]

Robin Morgan, usually able to keep above the fray, responded to defend Steinem in a rather back-handed way. Morgan claimed Steinem was no radical, indicating that she had "never seen her as a raging feminist man-hating broom rider but rather as a whimpy moderate."[9]

Underlying this argument, of course, were very deep ideological differences over who was the enemy and what should be done. For Steinem, Friedan and Morgan reflected in their politics and writing the most essential differences in the movement. Steinem, while describing herself as a radical feminist, was not radical enough for Morgan, essentially because Steinem fostered a belief in electoral politics rather than revolution. Yet she was too radical for Friedan. Steinem never fully accepted but fostered the radical feminist position on "men" as the enemy. While never a separatist, she recognized the validity of the separatist and lesbian positions. In the narrow spectrum of feminist politics, Steinem was the classic liberal. The ideological differences went beyond these three figures and were played out in both the *Times* and the newly founded *Ms.*

Naming the Enemy

While women were discovering what it meant to be a woman, they were becoming less and less clear about what it meant to be a man. Just what role did men play in the

oppression of women? What role should they play in changing women's oppression? What role should they play in the
new society? All of these issues were increasingly troubling
to the movement as man became the enemy. What did it
mean to overthrow the enemy when the enemy was half of
the human race?

The idea that man was the enemy was first expressed
within the radical feminist community. Some radical
feminists argued for a separatist position, totally removed
from men. Also during this period, the lesbian movement
began to take shape. The radical lesbians emerged to not
only state their own sexual identity, but to put forward a
vision of society in which men could be eliminated altogether.

The intensification of the radical feminists' position led
Friedan to charge that "women can be guilty of chauvinism." She argued that:

> The assumption that women have any moral or
> spiritual superiority as a class or that men share
> brute insensitivity is male chauvinism in reverse:
> female sexism.[10]

Friedan argued that the movement would be "ir-
reparably damaged if we did not purge ourselves of female
chauvinism and begin to work with men instead of against
them." Friedan felt this way, not only because she thought
the anti-male image was alienating possible supporters of
the movement, but because she was convinced that it was
"inviting a backlash" that would endanger all of the real
gains the movement had achieved.[11]

Homosexuality

The issue of homosexuality, along with the divisiveness
created over naming the enemy, became volatile. "Sister-

hood" was invoked to mean that homosexuality and lesbianism had to be supported and endorsed by the movement. Controversy over the "morality of homosexuality" surfaced. This was compounded by the fact that it was precisely the charge that the movement was "nothing but a bunch of homosexuals" which had been so damaging in attracting working class and minority women. To now be asked to *actively* back the rights of lesbians and gays, and to welcome them publicly into the movement, seemed like suicide to many. On the other hand, radical feminists argued that the oppression of homosexual women was a "double oppression" in a heterosexually biased society. They held that the principles of the movement demanded support for lesbian women. To the radical feminist the lesbian personified the "free, liberated woman." Arguments became heated on all sides and by the fall of 1972 the *Times* reported that the "...issue of lesbianism was splitting the women's movement in New York."[12]

What Is to be Done?

Unable to agree on the enemy, the role of men or position of lesbians, the movement was less able to agree on tactics. Radical feminists wanted a more confrontive stance. The radical feminists coupled their attack on capitalism with an attack on partriarchy and talked of transforming the power structure and creating a "massive behavioural revolution aimed at overturning the very structure of a male-dominated society."[13]

While the radicals were talking about overturning society, NOW was trying everything to get *inside* and become part of the "mainstream." This was most clearly reflected in their stance on electoral politics. NOW not only backed candidates, it offered training sessions for women to run for office. One feminist spokesperson summed up the controversy, "there are women who just want a piece of the pie and then there are people who just want to change the pie."[14]

The Issues: Abortion and the ERA

In the course of all this dissension, two issues were framed that again gave focus to the movement. The first of these is abortion. Over the next few years the right of women to have abortions became almost synonymous with the women's movement. Perhaps no single issue has been more consistently discussed by either *Ms.* or the movement itself. In early 1972 Steinem gave one of the best statements of why the movement viewed the issue of abortion as central to the "liberation" of women. Wherever else Friedan, Morgan, or anyone else in the movement may have differed from her, on this issue there was widespread agreement. Steinem explained in her defense of sexual and reproductive freedom:

> We look at this as our Vietnam since there are more women dying from butchered abortions than servicemen killed over there....The right to abortion on demand is basic to female freedom.[15]

The commitment to the freedom of choice for women to have abortions was demonstrated in the very first "trial issue" of *Ms.* Magazine. Designed to see if in fact a magazine aimed at women concerned about the "movement" could reach a popular audience, *Ms.* decided to include a petition on abortion. Boldly headlined, a simple statement of belief appeared reading:

> I have had an abortion. I publicly join millions of other American women in demanding the repeal of all laws that restrict our reproductive freedom.[16]

This statment was of course made prior to the Supreme Court claim regulating restrictions on abortion. Women signing the petition were admitting to an illegal action. Along with the published names, a return blank was included so readers could send in their names as well. The goal was to present the petition to Congress. Throughout the first year of publication, abortion as an issue was kept before the readers. In their annual Christmas message wishing "peace on earth and good will toward people," *Ms.* expressed the hope for the new year that "only wanted children would be born into the world."[17]

The second major issue to appear with force in 1972 was the Equal Rights Amendment (ERA). In February of 1971, Bella Abzug and Martha Griffiths combined their efforts to get an equal rights amendment through the House. The ERA, proposed for nearly 50 years, was greeted with little fanfare. Senator Sam Ervin, later to become the darling of liberals based on his role in the Watergate hearings, remained true to his conservative position when being confronted with the ERA. He said simply, "the ERA is as wise as using an atom bomb to exterminate mice."[18] Yet neither the ERA nor abortion were all that significant to the movement. The tactic of consciousness-raising was the most important focal point of activity and the issues were just part of a larger range of items concerning the movement from day care to birth control, health practices to advertising and the media. But in 1973 all of that changed. The Supreme Court ruled laws prohibiting abortions unconstitutional, and the ERA, to everyone's surprise, became a symbolic referendum on the movement.

Organized Opposition

All of a sudden women found that they were embroiled in two of the most hotly contested issues to emerge in the

1970s. It was around the issues of abortion and the ERA that the opposition to the women's movement became not only most vocal but most organized. Anti-abortion and anti-ERA groups entered the scene of American politics with a vengeance.

The first discussion of the power of the opposition was noted in an article in *Ms.* Magazine. In April of 1973, Roberta Brandis Gratz wrote an article entitled "Never Again." This was one of the most controversial articles to appear as it was accompanied by the photo of a naked woman, left dead in a pool of blood by an illegal abortionist. Characterizing the woman as the victim of butchers, the theme of the article goes on to note that the death of this woman and thousands of others like her should never be allowed to happen again. Women were encouraged to struggle for repeal of restrictions on abortions (pre-Supreme Court decision). At this point Gratz notes the difficulties of this struggle because many "politicians quaked before the shrill outcries of the vocal Right to Life groups."[19] These vocal groups, the bane of politicians during the 1972 election, became all the more vocal and significant in the coming years.

The opposition to the ERA began in a more sophisticated fashion under the guidance of long time conservative political activist, Phyllis Schlafly. By 1972 Schlafly's STOP ERA drive had become so strong that *Ms.* devoted a special article to a discussion of her as the "sweetheart of the silent majority." Schlafly became responsible for promoting the arguments that the ERA would destroy families, legalize rape and send women into combat. She stood for the belief that to characterize the American woman as "downtrodden" was the "fraud of the century." In fact she argued that the "American women had never had it so good...she had the right to care for her own baby in her own home while her husband supported her."[20]

Thus the lines began to be drawn for the battle. The

ERA and abortion became wound together as part and parcel of the same thing—the women's movement, a movement which according to the opposition, was anti-life and out to destroy the very fabric of American society.

Victimization of Women

Underlying these two issues from the perspective of the movement was an assumption which helped to lend unity to their struggle. As women became more and more familiar with their own experience a subtle theme kept recurring. Somehow women were being victimized by the society— they were victims of the media, exploited for their bodies or buying power; victims of the health care industry, exploited as a way to push drugs or for guinea pigs for surgery; victimized by their families as unpaid labor; victimized at work by male bosses and a male-oriented system, victimized on the streets by the shouts, jeers and assaults of men and boys. This sense of victimization simmered through the early 1970s and came to fruition in the issue of rape.

Rape

Rape itself became a metaphor for the condition of women. The *Times* reported the comment that women were "raped on every date, raped by her husband, and raped finally on the abortionist table."[21]

This consciousness of sexual assault as an issue came slowly. The first discussion of it as a part of the agenda of activities of the women's movement occured in 1972. It happened as a response to legislation initiated in New York. The State Legislature was considering adopting a "corroboration ruling" in sex assault trials. The intent of this legislation was to say that a rape victim must be able to produce someone other than herself to corroborate her testimony. The notion behind this law was that most rape cases were brought about by women who had in some way "asked for it" or who were bringing rape charges to get "revenge on a man." The introduction of this legislation caused an immediate stir among the New York feminists. They said:

> The corroboration rule in rape before the New York State Legislature is clearly anti-feminist. Corroboration clearly is inimicable to feminists as it is to victims of forcible sodomy, the two are not mutually exclusive.[22]

And later the radicals elaborated what was to become the cornerstone of the feminist perspective on rape and sexual crimes "rape and sexual offense are enshrouded by sexual myths...[which] must be demythologized, recognized as aggravated physical assaults."[23]

Throughout the next few years women's activities across the country began to center on exploding the myths behind rape and establishing rape crises centers to encourage the reporting of rape by offering counseling and support to the victims. They also organized to update and revise traditional sexual assault laws to remove the onus placed on women who were raped. Rape was the only crime requiring the testimony of the victim to be corroborated by other witnesses before a criminal is convicted. Anti-rape activity had reached such nationwide proportions that *Ms.* devoted one of its departments, "How to Make Trouble," to a discussion of rape crisis centers and how to establish one in a local community.[24]

Emphasis on activity around the issue of rape came about based on a growing recognition by women of their vulnerability. As women explored their personal experiences, their relationships within their families, their work and their communities, they began to realize how much of their lives were shaped by the fear of physical or verbal assault. As a result, the concept of victimization opened up a new emphasis on the real biological limitations women faced. Women were forced to realize that "being a woman" was more than simply carrying out socially and politically ascribed roles. The biological reality of womanhood resulted in an ever present vulnerability which all women shared.

For some among the radical feminists, the acceptance of this biological aspect of their identity led to the creation of a new concept of women based almost solely on biology. Jane Alpert, while still a fugitive, published her letter to her sisters of the Weather Underground explaining her "conversion" to "radical feminist" based on her experiences as a woman while traveling across the country underground. She argued that she had come to see "biology" as the *source* not the enemy of the revolution. Thus she developed the theory of Mother Right.[25]

For other women the resurgence of the recognition of the biological basis of the female identity began to open a host of new questions about the relationships between nature and culture, between technology and humanity. Infusing arguments around medicine were perspectives on the earth and nature. Feminists started to explore age old questions from a new direction. Developing a feminist perspective enabled women to challenge many of the clinical, scientific, determinist, disposable notions deep within our culture. The best expression of this perspective has been developed most recently by Caroline Merchant in her work: *The Death of Nature*.[26]

Battered Women

These philosophical probings took time and evolved slowly. The movement, more focused on action, began to not only be concerned about rape, but about all physical violence toward women. Battered wives came out from behind closed doors.

In 1974, *Ms.* published its first report on domestic violence. Interestingly, this report was filed under their international section. It was a detailed description of the overwhelming response of women in London to a domestic violence shelter.[27] It was not until 1976 that domestic violence received full coverage as a phenomenon inside the U.S. Devoting the major focus of the August 1976 issue to battered wives, *Ms.* no doubt was reflecting the growing consciousness in the movement of violence as well as the actual activity around the establishment of shelters. Yet even at this point it was clear that the issue of domestic violence was just beginning to seep into the American consciousness at large.

In the lead article entitled, "One of these Days—Pow Right in the Kisser: The Truth about Battered Wives," Judith Gingold indicated how casually violence against women was regarded. She also demonstrated how the exploration of the issue of rape as a crime of violence rather than of passion enabled women to begin to have a new understanding of "wife beating." After a series of gruesome and gory accounts of women who had been beaten by their spouses, she commented:

> Reports like this are atrocious, inhuman, and all too easy to dismiss. Surely beating wives, like burning witches, is an archaic aberration, a cruelty only the deranged could commit or endure.
>
> In fact wife beating is among the most commonplace of crimes...
>
> Nevertheless, the plight of the abused wife has generally been ignored in our society. Assaulted wives have been convinced their ordeal is freakish

and shameful—or their own fault. Increasingly, however, these women are beginning to realize that they are not singularly cursed but victims of a more prevalent crime than rape—and just as misunderstood.[28]

As the personal accounts of their lives began to lead to disunity based on ideology and differences of race and class, they also began to expose a basis for a new unity growing out of their common victimization. Sexual assault, sexual harassment on the job and violence in the home became realities to be analyzed by women and programatically addressed.

This unity of program and purpose is perhaps most clearly seen in the attention paid to the rape cases of Inez Garcia and Jo Anne Little. Both the *Times* and *Ms.* commented on the development of these cases. *Ms.* devoted a special issue to a discussion of rape and the cases of both women.[29]

Both cases, while different, had certain similarities that enabled them to unify women. First Garcia and Jo Anne Little were both poor, minority women. Garcia was an illiterate Latina woman who had spent much of her life as a migrant worker. Jo Anne Little was a black woman from North Carolina where she had a history of petty crime. As such both women stood as a symbolic testament that the issues of the women's movement were no longer white and middle class. They transcended these categories to essential elements of being female. The symbolic importance of this to the movement became clear in the treatment of the Garcia case. A panic swept throughout the feminist community when it appeared that Inez Garcia might not have been "poor and uneducated." When money materialized for her bail, rumors abounded that Garcia was really the daughter of "wealthy Cubans in Miami" (not exactly a fitting symbol for the movement). Feminists quickly investigated the "charges of literacy and wealth," only to find them false. Gratified, they again united in the pursuit of justice. Thus both women, Jo Anne Little and Inez Garcia, provided a much needed symbolic unity. And feminists from all perspectives agreed on the importance of their cases.[30]

The second equally important symbol they represented was that both women had fought back. While victimized by men, they were not defeated by them. In the account of Inez Garcia we find this account:

> It happened one March night a year ago in Soledad, a dusty, windy California town that had sprung up around a prison the way highway towns do around gas stations. Miguel Jimenez lay dead in the street, and a suspect, Inez Garcia was arrested. She admitted the murder. She had gone after Jimenez and his friend...with a rifle, she said, and had gunned down one of them.[31]

The case of Jo Anne Little was strikingly similar. Little, who had been arrested for a minor offense was sexually assaulted by her white jailor. In the course of the assault, she grabbed the ice pick he had carried into the cell, stabbed him to death, then fled.

In both trials, the women admitted they had killed their attackers. They justified this by the fact "they had been raped."

These cases not only provided a basis of unified action through defense funds, discussion groups, support demonstration and actions, they became central to how women began to reconceptualize rape. In the simple words of Inez Garcia, women began a long struggle to separate rape from passion and to have it viewed as a crime of violence. As Garcia said in her own defense, "To me, what he did to me was an act of violence."[32]

The separation of rape from passion established an important theoretical concept. For the first time people were able to seriously question what sexuality and sexual activity meant in a way that had heretofore been impossible. The recognition of the relationship between sex, power and domination took on a much deeper meaning. The original distinction made years before by Kate Millet in *Sexual Politics* became vivid in the description and actuality of the lives of thousands of women. Additionally, this distinction opened up a new dialogue on the essence of sexuality itself.

As a nation we have never been known for the maturity of our discussion and treatment of sexuality. Shrouded in Puritan upbringing, and filled with taboos, or crudely and crassly commercial, issues of sexuality are either "not mentioned" or become a source of profits or jokes. As one feminist commented, "we are a country that has arrived at decadence without passing through maturity."[33] Yet through the exploration of the issue of rape, for the first time men and women began to make distinctions and separations about sexual activity. It was discussed not only in terms of power and profit, but in terms of affection, intimacy and reproduction.

Pornography

The importance of this new ability to talk and think about sexuality had an enormous impact on the movement. In the late 1970s women began to confront issues of pornography and the exploitation of people solely for profit.

Pornography has long been a complicated question in America. And especially so for the liberal or radical. Long accustomed to right-wing book bannings and burnings, the ability to "tolerate" and in fact support artistic expression has meant the willingness to forgo any effort at dictating standards for art. With the "sexual revolution" in the 1970s, this became all the more so. As Robin Morgan points out describing her own experience during her involvement in the new left:

> That was the period when I could still fake a convincing orgasm, still wouldn't be caught dead confronting an issue like pornography from fear...of being [a] bad vibes, up tight, un-hip chick.[34]

For intellectuals protecting the "first amendment" or individuals wanting not to appear "square", pornography was off limits to liberals. It was radical feminists who were the first to react to pornography. As early as 1970 Morgan and a small group were arrested for staging a protest in front of a theater.[35] But it was not until 1976 that the issue became legitimate within the movement and a focus of widespread outcry. In that year a new phenomenon hit the pornographic film industry—Snuff. Snuff films were selling for $100.00 a seat. The attraction? While keeping all the accoutrements of a traditional porn flick, Snuff added the dimension of actually killing the victim right on camera. Rumored to be using women kidnapped in mysterious Central American countries, these films reflected real brutality and death to real women. Outraged, women's groups began to picket the theaters to demand their closing and the elimination of this kind of material.[36] The *Times* called pornography the "new terrorism."[37]

Having been shocked into the recognition of the violence underlying much of the pornographic industry by this extreme expression, women began to look more closely at the whole subject. It seemed easy to understand the hideous nature of Snuff. Equally uncomplicated, and the next area of investigation, was the issue of child pornography. Still dominated by liberal concerns, the actions of consenting adults was one thing, but the inclusion of children into explicit sexual acts was a violation of the adult responsibility to nurture and protect the young. Quickly this exploration against the backdrop of the growing understanding of the relationship between sex and violence, women began to see that pornography was another form of power and domination. *Ms.* devoted the lead articles and feature section to an exploration of child pornography. Gloria Steinem in the introductory feature extended the argument saying pornography had nothing to do with sex or moral prudishness. She entitled her article: "Pornography—Not Sex but the Obscene Use of Power."

In the course of the article she begins to draw the separation between sexuality and the brutality and humiliation portrayed on the screen or in magazines:

> The truth is that sexuality itself isn't the source of the almost unbearable feelings of outrage and vicarious humiliation that brings tears to our eyes—and a frightening desire for revenge to our hearts—when we look at pornography, whether the object is an adult or a child. It is the obscene use of power, the physical or psychic violence done to one human being by another, the pleasure of the powerful in the humiliation and dehumanization of the powerless—that is the source of the outrage.[38]

Articles on incest and child pornography were given a high profile in *Ms.* and culminated in the November 1978 issue. The cover proclaims "Erotica and Pornography, Do You Know the Difference?" Acknowledging the dangers inherent in labelling things obscene, Steinem went on to talk about the distinctively human capacity for sexual activity not related to procreation. Noting that this distinction was often used by the Far Right to justify women's place as reproducer she states:

> Defending against such reaction...leads to another temptation: merely to reverse the terms, and

declare that all nonprocreative sex is good. In fact, however, this human activity can be as constructive or destructive, moral or immoral as any other. Sex as communication can send messages as different as life and death; even the origins of "erotica" and "pornography" reflect that fact. After all "erotica" is rooted in "eros" or passionate love and thus in the idea of positive choice, free will, the yearning for a particular person....Pornography begins with a root "porno," meaning "prostitution" or "female captives," thus letting us know that the subject is not mutual love, or love at all, but domination and violence against women.[39]

This distinction did not remain on the theoretical level, but helped to propel the formation of countless groups under the names of Women Against Violence Against Women and Women Against Pornography. Book stores became the targets of browse-ins, often forcing closure. Billboards and record albums picturing women in dehumanizing ways were forced to be taken down or recalled. Musical groups were picketed with song lyrics, often unintelligible to the young listeners, distributed so that people would be aware of what was occurring.

In city after city, begining in 1979 with a march of over 7,000 women, Take Back the Night marches began to be organized. Women were no longer willing to accept the status of vulnerable victims. They were organizing to confront pornography and rape.[40]

Thus throughout the late 1970s we saw the emergence of the women as victim metaphor. The metaphor grew out of the experiences of daily life that had been the earlier substance of the movement. These experiences enabled women to confront their own identity not in terms of contrast nor in terms of culturally or socially determined roles. Rather, women began to look at the relationship between their own biological nature and the society in which they lived. In the course of doing this, women made some of the most important distinctions in our understanding of our roles as human beings and to the expression of our sexual identity. Realizing that sex had been surrounded by myths and half-truths, removed from serious discussion or scrutiny, in the course of struggling against rape, domestic violence and pornography women began to separate sex from passion. They recognized sex had become associated with violence and domination. Having made this separation, it was possible for women to then make the distinctions between erotica and pornography and then to initiate activities directed at combating this kind of exploitation.

Marge Piercy, in the introduction to *Take Back the Night*, a collection of women writing on pornography, explicitly establishes the need to once and for all separate sexuality from violence:

> We live in cities like the tame pheasants who are hand-raised and then turned loose for hunters to shoot, an activity called sport. The hunting, maiming, the mutilation and murder of ourselves, our mothers, our grandmothers, our daughters, our granddaughters, is the stuff of a vast industry ....The link between sex and violence must be broken in our generation and broken for good if we are to survive into a future fit for our children to inhabit.[41]

The Breakdown of the Metaphor: End of a Movement

The 1970s saw another type of action as well. While women were exploring issues of rape, domestic violence, sexual harassment and pornography, the movement found itself pulled toward electoral politics. Almost all of the coverage in the *Times* in the late 1970s deals with the involvement of women in political issues and campaigns. *Ms.*, while giving voice to radical feminist and revolutionary women, nonetheless makes it clear it is primarily concerned with electoral issues. Discussing candidates, encouraging voting and highlighting women elected officials became standard features. The movement as a self-developing, explosive force in American life began to shift into the established institutions.

The primary activity changed dramatically. Grant writing to fund shelters and crisis centers became important. Lobbying for abortion legislation and the ERA were promoted. The direct political participation of women in actively discussing and deciding issues and tactics was replaced by those with skills to write proposals, run centers or lobby effectively. The "old activists" whose emphasis was on organizing, discussing and demonstrating began to fade away.

In 1975, marking the period of "Half-way Through the Seventies," *Ms.* did a retrospective on the movement. Robin Morgan, in an optimistic piece revealed some of the reality of this shift. She began her article by contrasting herself with some of her sisters. Musing in the mirror she comments:

An oldie...It is a species now endangered: often burned out, weary, cynical, embittered, and prone to seizures of matronizing advice for younger sisters. Yet this particular specimen is still active, hopeful even, and the face that looks out from beneath a few more proudly exhibited gray hairs each day, the face is almost—good grief—*mature*.[42]

Houston

For a moment in 1978 at the NOW convention in

Houston, it seemed that many of those who had been "burned out" were reignited. *Ms.*, never all that pleased with NOW, called the convention "Four Days that Changed the World." The *Times*, a little less excited, tried to assess feminist gains and losses. On the gains side: a three year extension of the ERA, pregnancy disability bill, aid to displaced homemakers, more part-time jobs, greater access to sports, and relief for farm widows. The set backs, however, were impressive: abortion had been restricted, shelters were denied funds, social security for homemakers was denied, child care was restricted and many old rape laws had resisted changing, as had many of the attitudes about rape. The *Times* and *Ms.* agreed that for the first time, the gathering was not all white and middle class. *Times* used the phrase "a rainbow of women: racially and economically diverse."[43] And *Ms.* was struck by the racial and ethnic diversity. Just as it seemed that on the surface race and class differences might have finally been transcended, so too it seemed that the issue of homosexuality, which had been so divisive throughout the last period, would be put to rest. The convention passed a resolution endorsing the right of individuals to their sexual preference. Under the new leadership of Ellie Smeal, a respected and thoughtful leader, it also seemed possible to reach the "housewife" Smeal typified. NOW moved forcefully to concentrate its tactics on the passage of ERA. In the course of this it solidified its ties with traditional electoral politics and practices. Over the course of the next few years, experiencing bitter and often unexpected defeats, the fight for ERA became transformed into a national referendum on the movement and NOW became the champion.[44]

As a result NOW more and more was wedded to the electoral arena. This is most clearly seen in the reaction of NOW to the defeat of the ERA. Its response, bitter and disappointed, was to simply target their own congressmen and women and get them elected. As a result, NOW in the 1982

1982 elections found itself in the curious position of backing male candidates running against feminists. This was based on the belief that the source of change was no longer the talk and action of men and women in their own lives, but the kind of laws and bills that could be passed in Congress.

Consequently, by the beginning of the 1980s a large force in the movement had ceased to exist as a social movement and became another interest group in the larger field of electoral politics. Nowhere is this more clearly reflected than in the *New York Times* editorial. Never one to devote editorials to women, the *Times* in August of 1980 commented that for years women had been "seen as extremists and troublemakers." But, it declared, at last they had become an "effective political force." Lauding praise for this accomplishment, the editorial concluded:

> The battle for women's rights is no longer lonely
> or peripheral. It has moved where it belongs: to the
> center of American politics.[45]

Thus by the beginning of the 1980s the women's movement as a force to question society had ceased to exist. While offering vital ideas and explorations, the movement no longer posed a challenge to the direction or fabric of American life. It had become a part of electoral politics. Women were no longer outsiders.

NOTES

1. "New College Trend: Women Studies," *New York Times*, 7 January 1971, p. 37.
2. "Job Bias against Women Easing under Pressure," *New York Times*, 31 January 1971, p. 50.

3. Israel Shenker, "Is It Possible for a Woman to Manhandle the King's English?" *New York Times*, 29 August 1971, p. 58.

4. Judy Klemesrud, "Women's Revolt? Harris Poll Detects 'Real Storm Signals,'" *New York Times*, 19 January 1971, p. 32.

5. "200 Black Women Have Dialogue," *New York Times*, 10 January 1972, p. 7.

6. "Older Women—Their Own Cry for Liberation," *New York Times*, 6 June 1972, p. 34.

7. A Personal Report on *Ms.*, *Ms.*, July 1972, Vol. 1, p. 4.

8. *New York Times*, 11 February 1972.

9. "Feminists Rebut Friedan Charge," *New York Times*, 20 July 1972.

10. "Feminists Scared by Betty Friedan," *New York Times*, 19 July 1972, p. 14.

11. Ibid.

12. Enid Henry, "The Movement...Is Big Enough to Roll with All These Punches," *New York Times*, 2 October 1972, p. 46.

13. Dieche Carmody, "Feminists Shift Emphasis from Persons to Politics", *New York Times*, 2 August 1972, p. 33.

14. *New York Times*, 20 July 1972, p. 29.

15. *New York Times*, 30 July 1972, VI, p. 14.

16. *Ms.*, Spring 1972, p. 34.

17. *Ms.*, December 1972, p. 39.

18. "House Accused of Bias as Hearing on Women's Rights Open", *New York Times*, 25 February 1971, p. 26.

19. Roberta Brandis Gratz, "Abortion Victims: Never Again," *Ms.*, April 1973, p. 44.

20. Lisa Cronin Wohl, "Phyllis Schlafly: The Sweetheart of the Silent Majority," *Ms.*, March 1974, p. 54.

21. *New York Times*, 30 July 1973, VII, p. 1.

22. *New York Times*, 27 February 1972, p. 24.

23. Ibid, p. 25.

24. "How to Make Trouble—Rape Crisis Centers," *Ms.*, September 1973, p. 6.

25. Jane Albert, "Education of a Feminist at Large," *Ms.*, August 1973, p. 52-59.

26. Carolyn Merchant, *The Death of Nature*, (San Francisco: Harper and Row, 1980).

27. Gay Seach, "Notes from Abroad: Battered Wives in London," *Ms.*, June 1974, p. 24.

28. Judith Gingold, "One of these Days—Pow! Right in the Kisser: the Truth about Battered Wives," *Ms.*, August 1976, p. 51.

29. Nan Blitman and Robin Green, "Inez Garcia on Trial: Rape Vic-

124

tim or Murderer," *Ms.*, May 1975, p. 49 and Angela David, "Forum: Jo Anne Little," *Ms.*, June 1975, p. 74.

30. Blitman and Green, p. 49.

31. Ibid.

32. Ibid, p. 88.

33. Molly Haskell, "What Is Hollywood Trying to Tell Us?" *Ms.*, April 1977, p. 49.

34. Robin Morgan: "Forum: Rights of Passage," *Ms.*, September 1975, p. 75.

35. Robin Morgan, "How to Run Pornography out of Town," *Ms.*, November 1978, p. 55.

36. Lindsay Van Gelder, "When Women Confront Street Porn," *Ms.*, January 1980, p. 62.

37. "Women/Pornography," *New York Times*, 4 December 1978, IV, p. 10.

38. Gloria Steinem, "Pornography—Not Sex but the Obscene Use of Power," *Ms.*, August 1977, p. 43.

39. Gloria Steinem, "Erotica and Pornography: A Clear and Present Difference," *Ms.*, November 1978, p. 54.

40. Lindsay Van Gelder, *Ms.*, January 1980, p. 64.

41. Marge Piercy, "An Open Letter," in *Take Back the Night: Women on Pornography*, edited by Laura Lederer, (New York: William Morrow and Company, 1980), p. 7.

42. Robin Morgan, *Ms.*, September 1975, p. 74.

43. "Houston Plus One Some Progress," *New York Times*, 18 November 1978.

44. Leslie Van Gelder, "Four Days that Changed the World: Behind the Scenes at Houston," *Ms.*, March 1978, p. 52.

45. "Storm over Women's Rights," *New York Times*, 20 August 1980.

CHAPTER VII

The Counter Movement

Social movements arise in conflict. Human beings who have been excluded from the political world come together to collectively change the institutions and values of their society. In the course of struggling to achieve a new reality and ideals, they challenge the existing power structure and provoke previously silent forces into action. Thus no social movement enters the political scene on its own terms. It is shaped and directed by the dialectical tension created with the status quo and the emerging counter movement. In fact the importance of a movement is often marked by the appearance of its opposition in the political world.[1]

The contemporary women's movement is no exception. It certainly has opposition. The very first questions raised by women in the 1960s brought down ridicule and laughter. The status quo attempted to silence its critics through humor. Very quickly, however, the reluctance of the general society to reassess itself was compounded by the development of organized opposition to the feminists. This organized opposition, often called the "new right," has taken particular aim at the women's movement and all it represents. As Roberts and Kloss point out, for the "new right" (reactionary right), the contemporary women's movement has come to symbolize a threat to basic values and institutions. The movement must be stopped.[2] The effort to stop the movement centered on the ERA for much of the last two decades. Roberts and Kloss note how anti-feminism formed the cornerstone of the reactionary right's ideology:

> ...the most powerful issues open to the reactionary right are anti-feminist concerns. These concerns focus around the efforts of the feminists to attach an Equal Rights Amendment (E.R.A.) to the Constitution of the United States. Phyllis Schlafly, the leader of the E.R.A. opposition, argues that American women are a "privileged group" and therefore, should hang onto their privileges.[3]

The E.R.A., however, was but a symbol of the deeper belief by the "new right" that the women's movement was threatening the very foundation of American life, the family.

Out of the tension between these two forces some of the central issues of the last two decades have been formed and debated within the halls of Congress, the streets of many towns and villages and in homes across America. It is a struggle the women's movement has been losing. This chapter looks at the interaction between the women's movement and its organized opposition.

Loyal Opposition

From the very beginning the women's movement faced

opposition. In the most general sense, the simple fact that the movement was attempting to develop a definition of women different from that held by the general society meant there would be inherent opposition. And given women's status and position in America, much of the opposition in the early days of the movement took the form of laughter. Whether in the halls of Congress, the corridors of SNCC or the privacy of the bedroom, the discussion of women's rights and responsibilities was frequently met with a snicker or a joke. Along with the joking and humor, there were serious theoretical attacks as well. Typical of these was the characterization of feminists by some contemporary psychologists. In clinical, detached language we are given the diagnosis of feminism as a disease:

> Militant liberationists can be traced to an initiative awareness of the militant's anger which springs not as she believes and would have us believe from her experiencing of the very real injustices which she describes, but rather from her own terrible fear, largely unconscious, that she, as a women, must destroy her very nature in order to attain full equality with men.[4]

In the beginning of the 1970s, however, the character and intent of the opposition changed dramatically. Women found themselves in direct confrontation with another emerging political force.

In many ways the New Right is neither "new" or "right." It claims its origins from the conservative theory developed during the 1950s. This theory rests on two major premises: 1. the necessity of confronting the expansion of big government and 2. the importance of confronting communism as the mortal enemy of America.[5]

These two basic ideological issues framed the backdrop around which a group of young conservatives began to meet and organize. Beginning in 1960 with a decision to work toward shifting the Republican party to the right, these conservatives began to work within party politics in earnest. In 1964 the Goldwater nomination as Republican standard bearer marked their first visible success. And despite the tremendous defeat of Goldwater at the polls, the "New Right" began to see itself moving toward ultimate political victory. Out of the Goldwater campaign came the Young Americans for Freedom, an organization that proved to be a vital source of continuing talent and energy for New Right organizations.

The major distinctions between the old and the new right however, rests on the New Right's concept of political power and the creation of a new social agenda. The New Right, while victorious in electoral politics, itself a distinction with the "old," never intended to function solely in the electoral arena. The broad scope of its direction and intent is described by Samuel T. Francis, one of the leaders of the New Right and legislative aid to Senator John East of North Carolina:

> The New Right is the political expression of a profound social movement that reflects the dynamics of American society and that promises to dominate not only politically but also perhaps socially and culturally. The origins of the New Right in a social movement explain why its political message often appears to be incoherent, contradictory, or simplistic. What the New Right has to say is not premeditated in academic seminars, calculated with precision in the inner sanctums of tax-exempt foundations, or debated in the stately prose of quarterly and fortnightly journals. The contents of its message are perceived injustices, unrelieved exploitation by anonymous powers that be, a threatened future, and an insulted past. It is

therefore understandable that the New Right has less use for the rhetorical trope and the extended syllogism than for the mass rally and the truth squad, and that some of its adherents sometimes fantasize that the cartridge box is not an unsatisfactory substitute for the ballot box.[6]

As social conservatives, the new right did not see itself as maintaining society's values and attitudes. Rather it felt that contemporary American society had become corrupt and degraded. Its role was to develop the political power necessary to restore "morality" and "principle." The New Right, then, was in *opposition* to what it considered the value and character of the ruling elite. Francis established that the New Right feels itself ridiculed and attacked by those in power:

It is in its cultural and social ideologies and lifestyles that the new elite has developed what is probably the clearest indicator of its dominant position. The lifestyles, aspirations, and values of the current elite are bound together, rationalized, and extended by what may be called the "cosmopolitan ethic." This ethic expresses an open contempt for what Edmund Burke called the "little platoons" of human society—the small town, the family, the neighborhood, the traditional class identities and their relationships—as well as for authoritative and disciplinary institutions—the army, police forces, parental authority, and the disciplines of school and church.[7]

And as champions of these "platoons," the New Right developed a social agenda to combat the forces of moral decay. Central to that agenda were: the defeat of the ERA and the elimination of abortion. To the New Right, one of the fundamental goals of restoring morality to America was the strengthening of the family. And the family was being destroyed by the women's movement.[8] As outlined in their major theoretical work *We Are Ready to Lead*, Richard Viguerie states directly that the women's movement and all it represented must be defeated if Americans were to reclaim their families. Equating working mothers with the devastation of war, he comments:

> ...industrialization, wars, economic pressure and working mothers have all combined to deprive children of good parenting. And without good committed parents, there can be few healthy children. And without healthy children, a society soon loses its vitality.
>
> There is an urgent need...to make the family flourish again, to fight anti-family organizations like the National Organization for Women and to resist laws like the Equal Rights Amendment that attack families and individuals.[9]

Thus the women's movement became a symbol to the New Right of all that was wrong with America. As middle class, white and often professional, the movement represented the "cosmopolitan ethic" so repugnant to the "middle American." Their actions and ideas ridiculed and devalued the very things the middle American constituency of the New Right cherished. The women's movement's perceived contempt for values was expressed in their desire for abortions, considered murder by the New Right and by their emphasis on the ERA, considered the source of destruction of the American family. While the women's movement may have been unable to "focus on its enemy," the New Right had no such difficulty. Liberals were the source of the ills of America. The liberal women's movement its most vile expression. Long before the democratic party or traditional media thought that the new right constituted a political force, the women's movement was doing battle with the "truth squads" and anti-abortion forces.[10]

Anti-Abortion

As a result, *Ms.* provided constant coverage of the growth of the New Right. As early as 1972, *Ms.* noted that the anti-abortion lobby had been "scaring off" legislative support by their beligerent tactics.[11] In 1975, International Women's Year, Gloria Steinem did an interview with Dr. Kenneth Edelin. Edelin had been indicted by a Boston grand jury for the "murder" of a fetus, the result of a legal abortion he performed in October, 1973 at Boston City Hospital. Edelin and Steinem gave vivid accounts of how the doctor had been trapped by abortion foes. He had been assisted in the operating room by doctors and nurses known to be outspokenly anti-abortion. These colleagues helped develop the charges against him. The prosecution in the case brought in a series of "expert witnesses" who, over the objections of the judge, continued to refer to the fetus as baby. They produced the finest of the right to life photographs and succeeded in getting a guilty verdict. Both Edelin and Steinem realized the impact of the decision, not only on the personal life of Dr. Edelin, who would appeal, but on the ability of any physician to perform an abortion. In the course of what the physician considered a relatively low risk procedure, he/she could be indicted for murder. Thus while the women's movement talked of the "choice of women," anti-abortionists saw abortion as murder.[12] The battle began to be drawn between the "pro-choice" and "pro-life" forces.

The Edelin story was followed with an article exploring the limited availability of abortions. Noting that since

the anti-abortion forces had lost the Supreme Court decision, they had taken to other tactics to close down clinics
and discourage hospitals from allowing the procedure. At
the very moment when the women's movement was becoming more closely tied with the electoral system and rending
itself from widespread appeal, the New Right was expanding its grass roots system and willingness to emerge
citizens in all kinds of political activities beyond voting.
While abortions were technically legal, they were not easily available. In her article Spalding stressed that the court
sanction had:

> ...done little to dampen the fervor of anti-abortion-
> ists who continue to lobby and introduce legisla-
> tion that requires constant vigilance if we are to
> preserve the right to choose whether or not to be
> pregnant.[13]

In early 1976, a special article was devoted to the right
to life convention. Louise Farr in "I Was a Spy at a Right
to Life Convention: Anyone Who Disagreed With Their
Logic is Pro-Death," provides a vivid image of the convention atmosphere. In the course of her discussion, Farr puts
forward what is to become the movement's "official line"
on abortion—it is not much different than having a tooth
pulled or your appendix taken out. Farr, in discussing the
propaganda pictures prominently displayed in the convention lobby comments:

> Fetus specially selected, of course, to look like lit-
> tle dead babies. Very bloody, because blood's an ef-
> fective deterrent. It would probably be an equally
> effective deterrent if the Right to Life movement
> were fighting appendectomies.[14]

In addition to documenting and describing the propaganda techniques of the New Right, *Ms.* began to take note of the annual demonstrations being held in Washington, D.C. to commemorate the Supreme Court decision to legalize abortion. Starting with 10,000 people, the crowds grew to over 64,000 participants.[15]

Slowly in the course of these descriptions the New Right view of sexual intercourse began to emerge. For *Ms.*, a magazine of the liberal thrust of the 1960s, devoted much coverage to methods of birth control and gave no hint that it had any sympathy with the Puritan beliefs of an earlier era. Yet *Ms.* began to see that for the New Right, this information was patent decadence. The Right argued that birth control could best be practiced through self control. Somehow pregnancy was to become a punishment for those unable to restrain themselves. Recognizing this puritan, narrow strain, however, did not enable *Ms.* or its followers to become more effective in combating them. By 1978 *Ms.* reports instead the escalation of activity by anti-abortionists, including the firebombing of abortion clinics, the harassment and physical abuse of those who work in them and the increasingly violent nature of confrontations between anti-abortion and planned parenthood clinics, particular targets of these groups.[16] Finally by 1980 we have Steinem attempting to demonstrate through careful logic that the women's movement is not the same thing as the Nazis. The anti-abortion forces had so successfully established the analogy between abortion and murder that women were accused of genocide. Steinem was compelled to try and separate the "Nazi connection" by arguing that Hitler would really be on the side of the anti-abortionists. Whatever the power of Steinem's logic, the fact that she was forced to seriously attempt to refute the analogy speaks to how powerfully it had been used to advance the cause of anti-abortion.[17]

134

The ERA

The second most important symbol for the women's movement, and the target of the New Right, was the ERA. In the very early days of the movement, the Equal Rights Amendment was but one of a broad range of issues concerning women. But as the decade wore on, the ERA came to symbolize a national referendum on the role of women in society especially as the movement itself became more tied to electoral politics and the legislative process. Like the issue of abortion, opposition to the ERA was discussed in *Ms.* in the early 1970s. By 1974 an article appeared analyzing the importance of Phyllis Schlafly as the leader to stop the ratification of ERA. Entitled "The Sweetheart of the Silent Majority," Lisa Cronin Wohl does a thorough job of establishing Schlafly's connections in the New Right. Noting that she was the author of "A Choice Not an Echo," the book dedicated to helping Goldwater win the 1964 election, Schlafly was also thought to be a member of the ultraconservative John Birch Society. The tone of Wohl's article is to indicate that Schlafly just doesn't seem to want to "play fair in the whole thing." Schlafly continued to report charges against the ERA that she knew weren't true, to pass herself off as a simple housewife and to convince women to believe that the ERA will destroy families, legalize abortion and send women into combat.[18]

Yet this careful analysis didn't prepare Ms. Wohl for the real power of Schlafly and the anti-ERA forces. It came as much of a shock to Wohl as to anyone else that the ERA was defeated in New York State. Expressing her surprise and dismay in an article entitled, "The ERA, What the Hell Happened?" Wohl noted how the Schlafly forces were able to link ERA with abortion, homosexuality and bussing. As before, however, Wohl's emphasis was to lament the unfairness of the tactics of the Stop ERA forces, without ever attempting to really understand why they raised such fears and questions in the majority of voters, both men and women.[19]

Reflecting also the growth of Anita Bryant and the creation of her Save Our Children organization and the growing power of Jessie Helms, *Ms.* remained descriptive of the New Right. Obviously troubled by what it represented, frequently on the defensive, *Ms.* took the stance of pointing out inconsistencies, tricks and fallacies in their reasoning and argument. Yet all the while, it was the New Right who began to reach the women Steinem had once called "those who most need our movement."[20]

Finally in June of 1979 *Ms.* attempts an analysis of the motivation of the women in the New Right. Andrea Dworkin in "Safety, Shelter, Rules, Form, Love: the Promise of the Ultra Right," acknowledges the power the right had in attracting many "average" Americans and in defeating the women's movement and its most important issues. She goes on to offer an explanation for why "sisters" are attracted to its promises. Drawing upon the metaphor of Women as Victim, she concludes.:

> [the new right]...makes certain metaphysical and material promises to women that both exploit and quiet some of women's deepest fears. These fears originate in the perception that male violence against women is uncontrollable and unpredictable ...The right promises to put enforceable restraints on male aggression, thus symbolizing survival for women.[21]

Thus the New Right's offer of a stable social order capable of containing male violence attracts women.

To borrow a phrase from an earlier detractor of the movement, "Ah, come off it." Should this analysis satisfy us? Is it possible that the emerging power of the New Right and the extraordinary allegiance given it by women is the result of women's fears of uncontrolled male violence. I think not. Rather, the growth of the New Right and its ability to defeat the movement grow directly out of one of the movement's own greatest weakness—the inability to look critically at itself, at the conditions it has helped to create and at the impact they are having on the lives of the people.

The refusal of the movement to examine its own ideas critically emerged very quickly in its development. In part the absence of criticism was an intentional effort to guarantee that women would become confident to voice their own ideas and feelings without being "attacked" by men or women who had become skilled at male leadership styles. Yet in 1975, as a lone voice, Vivian Gornick posed the difficulty this created for the movement. She said:

> It often seems to me that doctrine and doctrinaire opinions in the women's movement have developed as fast or even faster than the feminist thought itself. Almost from the beginning—even as women began to narrow their eyes with insight and men to stir with guilty defensiveness, there has been a growing tendency within feminist ranks to practice the curious self-censorship that accompanies the creation of dogma.[22]

Gornick, who is primarily concerned with how this self-censorship affected literary criticism goes on to explain:

> ...many feminists reviewing work done by women seem to suspend the rigorous intellectual judgment they are clearly capable of and instead opt for lavish and embarrassingly *un*critical praise of their "sisters'" artistic efforts. Conversely, whenever some effort at objective, intellectual judgement results in qualified praise or even critical rejection of a work by a woman, it is immediately denounced as sabotage.[23]

This uncritical stance did not restrict itself to literary or artistic endeavors, however. It infused the thinking and acting of women. Women began to deny parts of their own reality and the reality of others in order to hold on to their beliefs in the importance of the feminist cause. The mirroring of this can be seen in the work of Lindsay Van Gelder. Van Gelder was a frequent contributor to *Ms.* She had a short piece in the March 1976 issue which focused on the defeat of the ERA in New York. Her column, a small insert, developed the theme that many women voted against ERA because of the media image of the women's movement. After very brief comments, Van Gelder devoted the main body of her material to quoting women she met who told her they were not voting for the ERA. Stressing that none of these women voted against ERA because they feared homosexuality, unisex bathrooms or any of the other arguments of the right, she provided the testimony of three women. That of Lilly Newman, a 33 year old housewife is representative:

> I'm not exactly angry, but an outsider...I think it attracts women who personally feel they've been done an injustice by society and they're angry. There's no warmth in their movement. I know they're intelligent women, but I don't feel they put enough value on the feminine role in the home. The women who stays home is preparing the next generation, but that's not respected.[24]

Van Gelder lets these troubling comments stand on their own. She never probes why the woman feels like an "outsider," or why she feels the movement doesn't respect her role as wife and mother. Yet it is precisely these feelings which attract women to support the New Right—feelings created in part by the very activity and ideas of the movement.

Two years later, however, Van Gelder presents an article on "Cracking the Women's Movement Protection Game." The article begins with the statement that she did not tell the "whole truth" about what she saw during the ERA campaign in New York. She goes on to explain that she is now:

...telling this tale because I'm not the only feminist in recent years to have sacrificed "the whole truth" on behalf of what seemed to be the protective public relations of the movement.[25]

She points out how feminists developed a position which excluded their own experience with reality, if the experience didn't fit with the accepted "dogma" of feminists. The most telling case cited is that of abortion. She commented:

It is, for example, near heresy in some feminist circles to acknowledge that abortion might be any more complicated than having a wisdom tooth pulled. Despite the fact that feminists have worked hard to provide clinic counseling for pre and post abortion trauma, such efforts have generally been behind the scenes.[26]

And finally, in confronting the possibility of having to have an abortion, Van Gelder confronts the inability of feminist theory to provide her with a way to grapple with the moral issue involved:

...I desperately wanted a feminist article, pamphlet, speech, anything that would let me have both the abortion and my own ambivalence...I wanted to deal with the moral balance sheet of abortion—not have to deny that one existed for me.[27]

Through Van Gelder, then, we can begin to see part of the

reason why the New Right was able to attract the "outsider." The women's movement as a whole was never able to see that it was by its very actions contributing to the climate which was denigrating the experience of so many women in the home and family. While never as "anti-family" as the right contended, the movement certainly never succeeded in according the kind of respect and trust to the "average American woman" who only felt scorned because of her inability to recognize her own "oppression."

In part this is because feminism as an ideology was never able to provide Americans with a way to confront the complex and confusing issues that began to unravel in the nation. To make judgments simply in terms of what issues meant for individual women was not adequate. Issues of families, children, unemployment, social responsibility, exploding technology, nuclear war and a host of others required a larger vision. The issue of abortion is an example of how restricted and narrow the perspective of the feminist became. In the real experiences of every day life, abortion is after all something more than a toothache. It has been one of the most severely contested issues in our society. To approach the questions as though it were purely a matter of individual decision requires a blocking out of reality, a narrowing of the field of judgment, a denial of how we are all influenced by the society around us. Yet it is precisely this kind of judgment that feminism began to demand. And no matter how inadequate or troubling, it is precisely to this need for a larger more expanded basis of judgment that the New Right appealed.

In the course of the interaction between the women's movement and the New Right the movement became shaped by its opposition. They key issues of abortion and the ERA were selected by the Right as targets and women, in reaction, found their scope narrowed by the fight. Thus the movement gave up the control of the definition of its goals.

In addition to the loss of control over goals, the movement also suffered from never having defined an enemy. For some it was men, for others patriarchy and for still others capitalism. Ultimately, in order to maintain unity, the movement gave up the effort to agree. This created a tremendous vacuum. As a result the New Right was able to define the enemy for the movement—they claimed over and over again that the women's movement was anti-family. Thus the movement not only lost control of its goals, it lost control of the public definition of its enemy. The Right succeeded in making a victory for women a victory over family. Thus throughout the course of the movement, unable to define or agree upon its own enemy, the women's movement was cast in the role of explaining and reexplaining that it was not anti-family. The New Right then accomplished more than mere ridicule or laughter. Through its opposition it took control of the direction of the movement and most importantly, publicly defined the enemy, casting the movement in a defensive posture from which it never recovered.

NOTES

1. Griffin, 1952, p. 199.
2. Ron E. Roberts and Robert Marsh Kloss, *Social Movements: Between the Balcony and the Barricade* (St. Louis: The C. V. Mosby Company, 1979).
3. Ibid., p. 199-201.
4. "Women's Lib Psychology," *New York Times*, 12 March 1972.
5. Jerry Falwell, Introduction in *The New Right: We're Ready to Lead*, by Richard A. Viguerie (Falls Church, VA: The Viguerie Company, 1980), pp. iv-vii.
6. Samuel T. Francis, "Message from *MARS:* The Social Politics of the New Right," *The New Right Papers*, ed. by Robert W. Whitaker (New York: St. Martin's Press, 1982), p. 66.
7. Ibid., p. 69.
8. Roberts and Kloss, p. 199.

9. Richard Viguerie, *The New Right: We're Ready to Lead* (Falls Church, VA: The Viguerie Company, 1980), p. 196.

10. Francis, pp. 65-76.

11. Gratz, *Ms.*, April 1973, p. 44.

12. Gloria Steinem, "The Questions No One Asked Doctor Kenneth Edelin on the Stand," *Ms.*, August 1975, p. 76.

13. Denise Spalding, "Abortions: Legal But How Available?" *Ms.*, September 1975, p. 103.

14. Louise Farr, "I Was a Spy at a Right to Life Convention," *Ms.*, February 1976, p. 77.

15. Annual Abortion Act, *Ms.*, February 1976, p. 77.

16. Grace Lichtenstein, "The St. Paul Firebombings—New Wave of Terrorism Against Abortion," *Ms.*, November 1978, p. 58.

17. Gloria Steinem, "The Nazi Connection: If Hitler Were Alive, Whose Side Would He Be On?" *Ms.*, October 1978, p. 88.

18. Lisa Cronin Wohl, *Ms.*, March 1974, p. 54.

19. Lisa Cronin Wohl, "The ERA: What the Hell Happened in New York?" *Ms.*, March 1976, p. 64.

20. Lindsay Van Gelder, "Anita Bryant on the March: The Lessons of Dade County," *Ms.*, September 1977, p. 75 and "Will North Carolina Save Us?" *Ms.*, April 1978, p. 60.

21. Andrea Dworkin, "Safety, Shelter, Rules, Form, Love: The Promise of the Ultra Right," *Ms.*, June 1979, p. 62.

22. Vivian Gornick, "Forum: Feminist Writers Hanging Ourselves on a Party Line," *Ms.*, July 1975, p. 104.

23. Ibid.

24. Lindsay Van Gelder, "The 400,000 Vote Misunderstanding," *Ms.*, March 1976, p. 67.

25. Lindsay Van Gelder, "Cracking the Movement Protection Game," *Ms.*, December 1978, p. 66.

26. Ibid.

27. Ibid.

CHAPTER VIII
CONCLUSIONS

The women's movement touched the lives of Americans. Its effects cannot be measured by the policies it won or lost, the programs it established, or even the books and insights it developed. In the course of countless struggles, quiet victories and defeats, the movement has shaped a new, more complete picture of what it means to be a woman. This new identity can't be captured in a single leader or a particular policy. It is subtly woven within the symbols and talk that gave the movement its life. It is an identity which gave meaning to the movement and can best be understood through the metaphors which emerged to provide unity and coherence to otherwise diverse voices and actions of women during the last two decades. Through the dominant metaphors the collective action of the movement expresses itself. This collective action not only challenged the beliefs and direction of the larger society, it transformed the actors. Step by step, as each metaphor emerged, focused the movement, then gave way to the next, women achieved a fullness that would have been unimaginable a generation earlier.

These metaphors were charted in the popular media as it attempted to describe and interpret the movement to the larger society. Yet they were not created by the media. Nor were they calculated by strategists in the movement. They emerged out of the efforts of women to describe and understand their experiences. They came from the collective effort to define feelings and ideas that had been shrouded in silence. In the course of these efforts, women struggled with one of the most basic aspects of language—to use that which is known to understand that which we are only beginning to perceive. Thus, these metaphors became powerful because they captured the new collective reality of women. In giving voice to this reality, they helped to shape the strategies, tactics and policies that became the mark of the movement. Yet they also conveyed a new sense of women's lives, experiences and purpose.

Beginning with the Women as Nigger metaphor in the early 1960s, women who were already politically active began to grope for ways to understand the disparity they were experiencing between their political ideals and their personal lives. The analogy with the civil rights movement became a way to interpret this experience and provided a means of responding to their condition. Concepts of oppression, exploitation, and second-class citizenship were used to shatter the notion of womanhood as a "privileged position." Women began not only to describe their condition in these terms, but to consciously adapt the strategies and tactics that had been so successfully employed in civil rights struggles. Thus women questioned their ascribed social identity. The passive, dependent female of the post-war era was buried under a flurry of energetic political action and organizing. Women began to question the way things were. And then they moved to reject them.

The Woman as Nigger metaphor provided the basis for

the first important questioning of the female identity. However, in the beginning it dealt almost totally with women in the political world—where women were clearly "second-class citizens." Much of women's lives, however, were less public. The home, the workplace, the office and relationships with men were all central to the concerns of women. This initial questioning of the public role did not stretch easily into the home. Yet it leant a sharpness to the criticism of the private world. Women weren't just second-class citizens, they were second-class. The extension of the metaphor, however, created as much confusion as it had provided initial clarity. The claim that women were "slaves" to the family or that "sexism" was just like "racism" became extremely difficult for many women to accept. Their experience demonstrated they were less than full citizens, but the world of home and hearth was more complex. Experience here was much more confusing. As a result, by the mid-1960s, the civil rights metaphor lost its power. It began to obscure experience rather than to illuminate it.

Even as it waned, the civil rights metaphor had opened up a new basis for looking at women's lives. Recognizing their oppression, women not only rejected their public role, they began to question their private role. In the course of this, the second metaphor emerged. Women realized they had been defined by the society as little more than appendages to men. They were objects, rather than subjects who could think and act independently. With the same fierceness with which they had attacked the restrictions on their political participation, women began to challenge the very essence of their relationship to men. They challenged the roles of wife, mother and helpmate and began to raise basic questions about the nature of sexuality and intimacy. In so doing, long-held beliefs about politics, history, art and culture were turned on their heads. The "women's point of view" emerged as a legitimate and long overlooked perspective.

Negation ultimately requires some positive response. Rejection demands a new affirmation. By the early 1970s with the insights unleashed by the Woman as Object metaphor, women totally rejected the male world and all it represented. In a very real sense, the completeness with which the Woman as Object metaphor had indicted the male world left women with little alternative but to look at themselves. By describing their own experience, understanding and evaluating it, women were able to construct a new positive. Thus, the Woman as Persona metaphor emerged to celebrate the experience of being a woman. This metaphor was marked by the most central strategy of the movement, the consciousness-raising group. Women used these sessions to explore the texture of their daily lives. This exploration unleashed extraordinary energy and creativity. Women embraced many of the roles and attitudes ascribed them by the society. Overcoming their earlier rejection of these, they redefined their experiences as positive. Motherhood, nurturance, patience, conversation and caretaking were attributes of women recast into positive, essential values for the future. Women began to see themselves as not only having made essential contributions to the past but as holding the key to a new more human future.

The joy of discovering the "experience of women" uncovered a diversity that was more than anyone had bargained for. Women's experience included more than motherhood, careers and nurturing. It included complex emotions, passions, events and feelings. Issues of sexuality, crudely understood and rarely discussed in our society in any sophisticated way, became major concerns. Homosexuality, rarely tolerated among men, became a fearful issue to many women. Division of race and class, obscured under global claims of sisterhood, became concrete as women tried to get one another to understand experiences that were alien and often frightening. Experience, commonly felt and shared, had created the bonds of sisterhood. Yet experience, troubling, distant and misunderstood began to shatter these fragile ties.

By the mid 1970s, however, a new experience common to all women was given form. The reality of the physical vulnerability of women to the escalating violence in our society provided a new basis for unity. Pornography, a subject perhaps as old as time, took on a new visciousness in the mid-1970s. Brutalization of women, through rape, abortion , beatings, was brought into the open. Women, no matter how rich or poor, young or old, gay or straight, shared the basic fear of being victimized in a society becoming increasingly barbaric. Thus the Woman as Victim metaphor emerged to again provide unity to the movement. A host of programs, projects and articles were developed to recast our concepts of sex, love and violence. Consciousness-raising gave way to the creation of shelters and support groups.

The recognition of this common vulnerability demonstrated the new level of consciousness women had achieved. They did not respond by returning to the image of themselves as passive and weak. Nor did they appeal to men for protection. Rather, the symbols that emerged during this period were typified by the Inez Garcia and Jo Anne Little cases. These women were symbols not only as rape victims—they were victims who had *fought back*. They represented a new understanding of women and their potential for independent political action.

By the 1980s, then, women had created a new definition of what it means to be female. This definition captures the essence of Burke's notion of identity for it reveals that it was only by collective participation in the public world that women were able to enlarge the public and private concept of what it means to be female. Whatever else they achieved, whatever policy or direction they take, women can no longer step back into the home, nor retreat from their hard won identity. Women have become established as political actors, responsible now for themselves and their futures.

On Metaphor and Movement

The analysis of dominant metaphors gives us a way to chart the evolution of the movement itself. While a beginning point of a movement is often easy to detect, the subsequent growth and development is less visible. Metaphors provide a method to trace both the evolution of the stages of movement and to recognize important shifts in ideas, strategies and tactics. Stages of the movement can be seen through metaphoric shifts and changes.

In the course of the women's movement, metaphors emerged out of the reality of women's lives and their efforts to make their new understanding of themselves intelligible to others. As the movement progressed, the metaphors ran through it like waves, each emerging to lend coherence and unity, peaking and then subsiding as another surfaced in its place. While each metaphor is separate and distinct, offering a new idea, posing different strategies and tactics, each also depends upon the other, growing up in response to the contradictions in experience that were in part created by its predecessor. Each metaphor builds upon and advances the previous one. The totality of the movement then is revealed through the series of metaphors that emerge, lend unity and then fade.

Metaphors also provide a systematic method for capturing the collective nature of the movement. Rather than defining the movement in terms of leaders or policies, the metaphor provides an insight into the collective identity essential for the movement itself to coalesce and advance. The metaphor enables us to move beyond the prospective of the movement as a collection of individuals or struggle for policy and to understand the basis of the collective identity created in the course of the movement.

The use of metaphoric analysis then enables us to build upon the original insights of Griffin in a systematic way. The inception of the movement is clearly marked by the initial appeal for the creation of a collective identity—heretofore unrecognized by the society in a political sense. The rhetorical crisis likewise comes into sharper focus and we see it aimed both internally toward the movement and externally toward the larger society. Likewise the concept of consummation is able to be understood in terms of a state of being signified by the shift of the outsiders from a rejection frame to an acceptance frame.

Metaphors then enrich our understanding of the texture of movements. Rather than seeing a movement as a monolithic united whole, the metaphor reveals the essential ambiguities, and contradictions that weld together in the course of any effort for social change. They demonstrate how divergent, often contradictory ideologies and strategies can force a central basis for unity made possible by the course of the struggle to challenge basic aspects of society.

Reflections: On Strengths and Weaknesses

American women have amassed a rich political experience. They have challenged fundamental concepts about human relationships. They have expanded and reshaped the boundaries between personal and public life; given new depth to the understanding of the relationship between nature and culture; rediscovered a past and traditions that have given a greater sense of dignity to everyday experience. They have been able to unravel myths and half-truths that have obscured notions of sex and sexuality; to separate sex from power and intimacy from exploitation. And yet, women have ceased to challenge the direction of America. They have ceased to ignite the imaginations of young men and women now entering a time in which they can play very different roles and lead very different lives because of their efforts over the last twenty years.[1]

Why? Is it that too many activists just got "burned

out" or pulled into the system? Were women out maneuvered by the truth squads, mailing lists and baby pictures of the "new right"? Is it that movements just have a natural "life expectancy" and this one expired? There is a part of a truth implied in each of these perceptions. But, in many ways, the movement's greatest strengths were also its greatest weaknesses.

First and foremost, the movement sought and achieved a feeling of unity among women. Painfully conscious of how women had been separated and isolated from one another, or competitive and destructive in those rare instances when they were together, women sought and established sisterhood. Sisterhood was indeed powerful. It invigorated women. It gave them the courage to stand up to the ridicule, laughter and hostility of men and even other women. It empowered women to continue to pursue a deepened understanding of what it meant to be a woman. At the same time, however, the desire for sisterhood became a way to supress the development of consistent leadership within the movement. It served to stifle critical debate and to obscure very real differences of race and class. In short, sisterhood became a little too powerful for the health and vitality of the movement.

Lack of Leadership

In the early beginning of the movement, women prided themselves in rejecting male concepts of leadership. Equality among women became the watchword. This was expressed in a number of ways. For example, chairpersons for consciousness-raising groups were rotated so that no one person would begin to control or dominate meetings. The amount of time each woman had to speak was often regulated by cards or "chips." Spokespersons to the media were often anonymous. Women who became identified as leaders were accused of seeking stardom and quickly brought back into the anonymous fold. Those few women who did surface found themselves isolated from other women or under attack. The movement confused spokespersons and male styles of dominance with leadership. Thus the essential functions of leadership could not be developed within the confines of the movement.

The movement created a lot of activity and a multitude of organizations but there were no forms or processes for the collective evaluation of these activities nor for the development and refinement of strategies and tactics. These essential leadership functions were buried under the demand for equality. Moreover, on a conceptual level, the creation of ideas to advance the movement and to consistently challenge the prevailing philosophy and ideology of the power structure depended on individual insights rather than systematic collective processes. The leadership required to observe, distill and then formulate experiences into advanced ideas was never allowed to develop. It was consciously suppressed in the name of equality. As a result, spokespersons and administrators emerged. Consistent, evaluative, reflective and challenging leaders were inhibited.

Lack of Critical Debate

This equalitarian impulse underlying the drive for unity also served to stifle serious criticism. Women recognized and acknowledged sharp theoretical differences emerging in the movement, but they rarely challenged any given set of ideas. Somehow all ideas and theories were treated as equally valid and above critical analysis. Lack of critical discussion is always dangerous in political action. But it becomes all the more so when attempting to challenge fundamental concepts about human society. Nowhere is the confusion over ideas clearer than in the development of the issue of the family. The Woman as Nigger metaphor had some legitimacy in the public world. As it was stretched into the private world of the home and family however, it became destructive to thought and actually denied much of the reality of the experience of many women. Particularly for African-Americans and for white working class ethnic Americans, who were later to become the forces for the new right, the family was not experienced as a source of oppression. Rather, it was a source of solace. While never the "haven in a heartless world" celebrated in American Myth, many Americans were profoundly troubled by the drastic changes tearing at the fabric of the family throughout the Post World War II period. The reality of the escalating divorce rate, of intergenerational conflicts, of the constant separation and estrangement made possible by the extraordinary mobility of the expanding economy disturbed people who had looked to the family for comfort. The family was literally falling apart. Certainly a source of tension, frustration and often brutality, the loss of the family represented one of the most painful realities of modern America. In the face of this, the equation of marriage with slavery and the family as a source of oppression was not only odious but it did little to enable men and women to confront and explore the new and confusing issues emerging in their lives. These issues, posed by the disintegration of families and the intense conflicts experienced as men, women, parents, children, workers and non-workers all trying to adjust their lives went far beyond the question of the role of women. As important as this question was, and as much as it needed an answer, it was simply insufficient to resolve the tensions people experienced. In fact it did little more than increase the fears of many Americans that the family was disappearing.

Perhaps no group has more understood and exploited the inability of the women's movement to provide a conceptual framework for discussing the family than the new right. For it was over the issue of the family, of which abortion and the ERA were but symbols, that many working class and minority women were unable to accept the movement. And over this issue the new right was able to mobilize its most active opposition to the movement.

Denial of Experience

Sisterhood also obscured the very real divisions of race and class in America. Certainly in the boundary busting 1960s, social class in many ways became obscure. Racism, if not eliminated, was at least driven out of the legal realm of respectability. Yet the attitudes of Americans toward sex and sexuality are inextricably bound up with our attitudes toward race. The heart of the American experience has been the entwining of these two issues. The appeal to sisterhood, rather than attempting to unravel this relationship served to deny the particular historical and social experiences of black women as distinct in American society. To discuss sex without confronting race obscured the connection between sex and violence.[2]

If one takes a moment to reflect on the reality of the existence of black men and women in the south prior to the civil rights movement, the link between sex and violence emerges starkly. The use of sex as a weapon of intimidation underscores the relationships between the races and reveals the twin taboos that have helped shape the American character. The history of lynchings in this country is as much a reflection of sexual fears as it is of racial antagonism. The case of Emmett Till, often looked upon as the beginnings of the civil rights movement, represented the lynching of a young boy for "raping a white woman in his mind." The daily tensions between blacks and whites marked by a strict social code that emphasized physical separation wound up our attitudes toward race and sex in an intricate system of beliefs, myths and fears. Meanwhile intimidation and terror through the exploitation of the sexual vulnerability of black women has long been fundamental to the relationships between blacks and whites. Yet the violence surrounding sex and race attracted little comment from the movement. It was not until white women in the larger northern cities began to recognize the reality of their own physical vulnerability and the pervasiveness of rape that the movement began to address the distinction between intercourse and intimacy. The reality of the unique experiences based on race and class differences, which might have illuminated this issue, were obliterated under sisterhood. Superficial symbols of unity such as Inez Garcia and Jo Anne Little surfaced as a rallying point to obscure the real conflicts in experience and oppression of women.[3] These symbols served more to illustrate to white middle class women that they were linked to all women regardless of race or class, than to attract minority women to the movement. Somehow the exploration of differences posed a threat to the biological concept of the female identity. The bonds of sisterhood meant a flattening of the intensely personal and sometimes divisive reality implicit in racial and class experience. A kind of "orthodoxy of experience" developed which required a further denial of real feelings and tensions. Some experiences just weren't talked about. If they were, there was a way in which they had to be addressed. The anxiety women felt when confronted with the questions of abortion, for example, had to be quickly covered over by arguing abortion was nothing more than having an appendix removed. The tensions felt when talking with or working with people of different races or classes were kept to oneself for fear of destroying sisterhood. Doubts raised about ideas and actions were suppressed out of fear of disloyalty to the "movement."

As a result, despite the courage in confronting difficult

questions of values, the only standard for social, political and economic judgments the movement developed was the simple question "what does this mean for women?" As important as this question was in establishing the identity of women as political actors, it is/was simply an insufficient basis upon which to address the complex questions raised in the 1970s and 1980s. This standard of judgment is too meager an intellectual and emotional framework to guide action. Despite Steinem's claim that anything affecting 51% of the population can't be viewed as a single issue—she literally misses the question. It is no longer sufficient to think of questions of nuclear war, of massive unemployment, of widespread crime and drug addictions, of the countless social and political crises we face everyday from the standpoint of what it means to women. The issues of the 1980s and 1990s require a larger philosophical outlook. They require not only an expanded understanding of our own personhood but an understanding of how that personhood is connected to the larger human community. It is this connection that the movement has yet to make.

The Shift to Electoral Politics

The movement also found itself increasingly attracted to the world of electoral politics. In part the emphasis on the ERA fostered this tendency. The ERA, after all, is an issue of electoral politics. It required having friendly legislators at both the state and national levels. Women found themselves turning from protesters and demonstrators into lobbyists and letter writers. After the defeat of the ERA in New York and the recognition of organized opposition, the ERA became a symbol not only to the "new right" but to the movement itself. Its passage became either a vindication of women's struggles, just as for the new right its defeat became an indictment of all the movement had hoped to achieve.

Yet the tie to electoral politics went far beyond the ERA. In the mid 1970s the activity of the movement took on a new character.Rape crisis shelters,women's study programs, self-help programs, "how to..." conferences, law suits, retraining of displaced homemakers, health care clinics and domestic violence shelters and a host of projects and programs became the focus of the work of the movement. And this new "work" was often underwritten by government grants. This became so much the case that *Ms.* developed a special cover story on writing and asking for money. The energy unleashed by women meeting and talking was replaced by systematic programs. Step by step the movement became tied to cultural or governmental foundations. The heart and soul of the movement, the talk and action of women challenging basic ideas and beliefs was transformed into women skillfully pressuring the system to give them a little more here or there. Activity became dependent on the ability to secure funds. Challenge was replaced by pressure.

In a subtle way the very creation of a new sense of female identity or consciousness helped to foster this activity. Politics in the 1970s was dominated by interest group action—each identifiable group attempting to secure a "piece of the American pie" for themselves. Women having created a new group identity, then began to conceive of themselves as just one more interest group among the many competing for their share. Thus the movement became a reflection of the liberal philosophy which had absorbed and underscored social change for over 50 years—politics was the art of attracting resources for your particular interest group, not discussing public, common interest.

Consequently, the movement no longer rejected the basic structure of society. It simply wanted to be recognized as an identifiable group large enough to be included in it. The shift to this acceptance frame is perhaps most clearly exemplified by the position taken by NOW in response to the decision by President Carter to reinstate the draft registration. NOW argued only that women should be included in the draft, not that there was anything questionable about the military policy and direction of the country. Radical women, who once talked of revolutionizing the society, found themselves increasingly tied to programs and policies funded or restricted by the federal government. The skills demanded for these activities both in securing funds and pressuring legislators were more and more those of the middle class, less and less those of the neighborhood organizer.[4]

This emergence of sisterhood and the understanding of women as an interest group made possible by the emerging female identity both firmly established women in the political world and yet also restricted the appeal of the movement. The standard of judgment implied by these achievements was too narrow to encompass the very real fears that women and men were beginning to express about their lives. For many women, the movement out of the home was frightening. And for many others, especially poor, working and minority women, work outside of the home had always been a reality. To suddenly have what for them had been a difficult and stressful situation elevated to the status of providing a new kind of liberation was absurd. The movement seemed to be speaking only to and for those women who had the option to work and the option for professional jobs. It reflected little understanding of those women who had always worked and raised families, and who now desperately needed some way to think and talk about the multitude of tensions they were experiencing.

The Opposition Framework

Thus the emphasis on the family as a restriction from personal fulfillment, the narrow standard of judgment offered, and the shift toward electoral, interest group politics further underscored the middle class, professional image of the movement. Consequently the movement became vulnerable to the attack of the new right. It began to represent the cosmopolitan elite, the amoral, unattached, self seeking "limousine liberals" who the new right identified as the epitome of all that is wrong with America.

And this equation was not entirely unjustified. As long as women chose to approach issues solely from the frame of reference of their particular interest group, the kind of depth and complexity which they could bring to the issues of the 1980s was severely limited.

In addition the new right has been able to shift the dialectical tension between the movement and its opposition by taking the initiative in defining the issues for struggle. The broad range of questions, the issues of family, work and sex that women initially raised, lost their complexity as the movement allowed the right to define the grounds on which the movement itself would be judged. The ERA and abortion issues were never central to the initial beginning of the movement. But as the movement responded to its opposition, as it more and more found itself in a defensive posture, it gradually gave up the exploration of other fundamental questions. It allowed the opposition to define the struggle. The movement narrowed not only its political base, but it narrowed its conceptual reference. Finally at the very moment when the new right began building grass roots roots organizations, drawing upon many of the fears and frustrations of men and women, particularly among ethnic Americans, the women's movement narrowed its parameters. Convinced that its activities would affect the lives of all women (which was to a certain extent justified) the movement ceased to struggle to create the political processes to engage larger numbers of women in action. The activity of the movement shifted into the electoral sphere. Electoral politics does not require a mass movement. On the contrary, it requires a few skilled and dedicated individuals. Thus the movement not only allowed the right to define the issues on which it would be judged, it gave over much of the potential constituency to them.

Incomplete Drama

This narrowing of issues and the restriction of the base of the movement goes deeper than a proclivity for electoral politics or seduction of the liberal philosophy. In a Burkean sense, the movement was never quite able to complete the drama it had began. The final act eluded it.

During the emergence of the Woman as Nigger metaphor there was a general agreement that women had entered a polluted environment. This metaphor, by drawing a contrast between the condition of women and the condition of blacks, was able to help define the essence of that pollution. Women began to agree that something definitely had to change. And as women began to discover the existing definition of women, the Woman as Object metaphor served as a basis for the rejection of that definition. Women would not continue to be treated and defined as something less than full autonomous human beings.

However, having come to terms with a polluted environment, women were never able to agree on the assignment of guilt. In fact, under the Persona metaphor, women actually abandoned the idea of needing to assign it. For some it was capitalism. For others patriarchy. For some it was men. Guilt was everywhere, and consequently nowhere. This held important implications for the emergence of the next metaphor: women as victim. In a sense, women took on the "guilt" for their own condition. Victimage implied an oppressor. Yet who was the oppressor of woman? Interestingly, the symbols of unity that emerged under this metaphor indicate how the confusion and dissension over the "oppressor" was resolved. Women became responsible for their own condition. And it was only those who "fought back" who were able to achieve redemption. The enemy became the "enemy within." It was this internal assignment of guilt which facilitated the movement's shift into electoral politics. Since "guilt" was not assigned to anything or anyone within the larger social system, the transition from "outsider," from a rejection frame to an acceptance frame, was conceptually possible. Women, by changing themselves, by fighting back were able to re-enter society. Redemption no longer required struggling against the system. It required struggling against ourselves to be willing to stand up and fight back. Thus the inability to agree upon the assignment of guilt to an external enemy in the larger society provided the basis for the gradual shift back into the system. It removed the necessity for ongoing confrontation between the movement and the fundamental ideas, values and policies of the power structure.

A New Drama

In reality, of course, the world women moved back into was not much like the one they denounced two decades ago. The very course of their denouncements, as well as the activity of the other movements in the later 1960s and early 1970s had shaken the foundations of American society. At the same time the transformation of American industrial power and the increasing military posture of the nation combined to present Americans with the most profound social, economic and political crisis in over 50 years. The liberal philosophy and programs which had so easily absorbed the "outsiders" from previous movements had lost the ability or willingness to continue to expand. The 1980s marked not only the failure of liberal policies and programs, but also the failure of the liberal imagination. For the first time in over half a century, the future of America has been called into serious question.[5]

At the same time, however, there is another reality. Women have changed too. They had a new definition of themselves. Women no longer needed to legitimize actions in terms of another. Nor do women think of themselves as passive objects or victims. Women have *in fact* achieved a new, more complete, identity, precisely because they challenged and changed the direction of our nation. Women have seen the power of their own actions and choices. And now, having achieved this new identity, women cannot retreat. Nor can we simply stop where we are. It is no longer sufficient to confront the host of complex and difficult issues unfolding in the coming decade with the simple question— what does this mean for women? Women should have learned the limits of this question. They now have a larger obligation. They have the opportunity to look not just to women and their rich history but to women as *political actors*. Personal and political lives are bound up with issues that touch not only women, but families, communities and our nation. We have before us the beginning of a new drama. A drama made possible by many of the questions left unanswered. And a drama made necessary by the profound choices we now have to make, no longer just as women, but as politically responsible human beings.

NOTES

1. Betty Friedan, "Twenty Years After the Feminine Mystique," *New York Times*, 27 February 1983, p. 35.

2. Lillian Smith, *Killers of the Dream* (New York: Norton, 1961).

3. Angela Davis, *Women, Race and Class* (New York: Random House, 1981), pp. 172-201.

4. Friedan, *New York Times*, 27 February 1983, p. 36.

5. Ibid.

EPILOGUE:
From Political Actor to Spirit Healer

A new polarization is emerging in our country as we approach the 21st century. Women are vital to its development by playing new political and economic roles. Those who continue to challenge the nature and direction of our country are weaving images and ideas that potentially can radically alter the texture of our lives. Those who uphold the system are becoming increasingly entrenched.

The movements of the 1960s and 1970s have established new political actors whose perspectives, passions and visions must now be taken into account as we fashion our public life together. Like the movement of African-Americans which gave it birth, the women's movement achieved a new sense of identity. Above all else, through the countless struggles of these last two decades, women have created themselves as human beings fully responsible for their own public and personal lives. We will no longer remain silent or hidden.

But our silence has not been broken with a single voice. Today the challenge is no longer to get women to speak. It is a question of what we are saying, what values we represent, for whom we speak, and for what purposes. Women are now a political force, providing much of the energy and talent to movements of both the right and the left.

Our voices are increasingly divided. Women who felt attacked and disregarded by the movement have become central to the development of organized efforts to restore women to their proper place. The resurgence of religious fundamentalism has attracted hundreds of thousands of women and men to an ideology that rests on the inferior position of women and their association with evil. Anti-abortion forces propose constitutional amendments, initiate state laws to restrict or eliminate abortions, picket abortion clinics and those who attend them, oppose any effort at sexual education and in many cases engage in direct and violent action. Schools, the traditional domain of women, are becoming battle grounds in the war to stamp out "secular humanism" as women lead fights against textbooks and "suspicious curriculae." Increasingly the public spokespersons for escalating militarism and "vigilance against the communists" are likely to be women as well as men.[1]

At the same time women have brought a new energy to progressive and radical politics. Anti-nuclear activities and disarmament strategies have been clearly influenced by women. We are playing key roles in anti-interventionist and Central American support activity. The emerging bio-regional movement and the national Greens movement embrace "eco-feminism." The Sanctuary movement overtly claims allegiance to feminist ideas. Women have become principle actors in direct action campaigns of all sorts from Mother's Day marches against armaments and nuclear testing to weaving banner webs around the Pentagon and reclaiming the Statue of Liberty as a feminist symbol.

And as has always been the case, it is women who are

providing much of the energy and action for community based struggles: be they the efforts of the Dineh at Big Mountain to retain their land or the countless community groups working with issues that attack the dignity of people struggling with the deterioration of modern life. Issues of child abuse, domestic violence, drug addiction, community health, housing, food supply, pollution, toxic dumps, rape, crime, social service cut backs, health care benefits, small farms, cooperatives, mortgage foreclosures, and education are grappled with in small towns, rural communities and urban neighborhoods throughout the country. These secular efforts are joined by church based activities making up the fabric of daily life. The energy and efforts of women are critical to the existence of all of these.

Surrounding this activity is the changing contour of American society. Sometimes called the post-industrial age, the information age, or the new technological society, the United States is entering the 21st Century with a two-tiered society. This is something new. While there has always been an underclass, this is the first time its existence has been not only acknowledged but accepted as inevitable. This change was noted in the recent *Chicago Tribune* study, *The American Millstone:*

> The existence of an underclass in itself is not new in this country. What appears to be different today from past decades and centuries is what gives every indication of being the permanent entrapment of significant numbers of Americans, especially urban blacks, in a world apart at the bottom of society. And for the first time, much of the rest of America seems to be accepting a permanent underclass as a sad, if frightening, fact of life.[2]

The dimensions of this underclass are staggering. From 1978 to 1983, nearly 11 million Americans fell below the poverty line. From the Bureau of the Census we find:

The poverty rate for 1984 was 14.4 percent, or 33.7 million people. Of those, 22.9 million were white (11.5 percent of the white population) and 9.4 million were black (33.8 percent of the black population. The poverty rate for people of Spanish origin, who may be counted as white or black, was 28.4 percent, or 4.8 million people.[3]

And in all groups, it is women and their children who are the majority of the poor. Today one out of every four children is living in poverty. Most often these are working women, raising families or elderly women suffering from fear and isolation.

Along with the acceptance of the underclass has come a second, equally important change. The very nature of work is being refashioned. High technology may not have brought high pay, but it has re-opened many of the doors of the factory and workplace once slammed shut behind Rosie the Riveter. We find:

Since the mid-1970s, the US civilian labor force has grown 21 percent. Working women account for more than 62 percent of the total growth, as their numbers have risen from 37 million to 50 million . . .

A record 54.5 percent of U.S. women over age 15 are working or looking for work in 1985. In the prime age group 25 to 54, nearly 70 percent were in the labor force.

By the next decade fully 60 percent of the nation's women are expected to be in the labor force, including almost 80 percent of those aged 25 to 54 . . .[4]

Behind all these statistics are the faces of real women

and their families. Women worried about paying the bills, getting through the day, spending time with their children, trying to work and do the laundry, caring for their families, waiting in lines, watching over births and deaths, becoming mothers and grandmothers too young and wondering what's it all about. Some give in or give up. Most live from day to day with a sense of compassion and courage.

Thus, by the mid-1980s, women occupy a central role in the political and economic life of the nation. But this role is far from the enriched position envisioned a generation earlier. The reality of the condition of women gives rise to the speculation that the women's liberation movement, after all, was not a communist plot. Rather, it was a capitalist, chauvinist plot designed ultimately to protect the patriarchy and to further exploit women.[5]

Does the emergence of Women as Political Actor mean only that women can join men in the pursuit of power and privilege or that we can become exploited in the world of work as well as within the home?

This question does more than point toward the limitations of the contemporary women's movement. It reflects the condition of any group in this century whose efforts at social change have stopped short of a fundamental transformation of our culture. Precisely this notion of cultural transformation gives us a glimpse of the role women can play in the late 1980s and 1990s. Woman as Political Actor is giving way to Woman as Spirit Healer.

This metaphor is just beginning to emerge in the mass media. In part this is because of the changing nature of the media during the 1980s. "Movement" activity of any sort receives limited and fragmented coverage. But it is also a reflection of a qualitative change in the kinds of actions women are taking which challenge the direction of the country. Having an impact on the more traditional political realms, the new fusion of politics and spirituality is taking place in small groups and gatherings going almost unnoticed by the dominant culture. Much of the creative force and energy is coming from the lesbian community, which is almost completely ignored by the media, except to be invoked as a means of "discrediting" the movement. But precisely because lesbian identity and integrity requires a fundamental change in society, they among all women have resisted the move toward incorporation into the predominant culture and are playing an important role in the creation of Woman as Spirit Healer.

This metaphor is fraught with promise and contradiction. It offers the promise of a completely new understanding of the relationship of the material and the spiritual world. Reaching back to images of a time before the development of patriarchal society, women are beginning to evoke a vision of the capacity of human beings to live with a sense of connectedness to one another and to nature. They offer a new concept of political power free from domination and control.

On the other hand, these philosophical and pragmatic insights hold the danger of being little more than a collection of ideas offering personal growth and individual salvation in a world increasingly hostile to the vast majority of women and men.

Recognizing the possibility of this expansive spirituality to become just one more element in the personal growth industries of the "new age," Sally Gearhart cautioned early in the development of this metaphor that spiritual growth can become removed from political struggle:

> But if we get too far into this attitude, we will not be political at all but only 'groovy,' 'far out' women, each doing her own thing and assuring each other every now and again that by living our mellowed-out lives we are thus doing our bit, creating the atmosphere, tra-la!, in which Toots and Amy and the governor's wife and the woman hanging out diapers

in Middle America are all someday going to blos-
som into feminists—re-sourcement feminists at
that. I suggest that unless we read and think and
talk and study and practice with our vision constantly in mind and with our political sensibilities
consistently sharpened, unless we somehow conceptualize that vision (knowing it will change) and
ritualize the expression of it, we may forget entirely that we are a dynamic force in history.[6]

Woman as Spirit Healer holds the potential for a critique
and rejection of modern society. But the ability to forge this
critique into a new social reality depends a great deal on the
capacity of women leading the way to tie this new vision
to the day-to-day struggles that form the lives of most
women and their families.

A Cultural Critique

Of all of the movements of the 1960s and 1970s, the
women's liberation movement was the most consciously
critical of contemporary culture. In part this is because the
movement evolved remarkably free from ideology. The progressive left's disregard for culture as irrelevant superstructure had little impact on it. And as a movement which
celebrated the experience of its members, it was forced to
confront patterns of thought, modes of action and interaction, media images, language, institutional structures and
ideas in fundamental ways. Everything from the liturgy of
the Catholic church to the plot line of the comic strips was
analyzed, criticized, explored and found "sexist." Whatever
the limitations or excesses of this criticism, an understanding of high culture, pop-culture and mass culture became
central to political and social action. This criticism expanded
our view of political and social reality and the forces that
shape our lives within it.[7]

The depth of the cultural critique rested on identifying the denial of the experience of women in the modern world. Searching out these roots ultimately led to an analysis of the basic values and attitudes which inform our life. And this led to religion and the religious myths and images which impart meaning.

Women began to re-view the origins of contemporary culture and to argue that the establishment of this culture on principles which distort our view of women and of nature is the source not only of sexism but of all oppression and of the attitudes and ideas that are leading us to the destruction of the earth. These values and attitudes are embodied in religion. Rosemary Reuther, one of the first to articulate this view, said:

> All the basic dualities—the alienation of the mind from the body; the alienation of the subjective self from the objective world; the subjective retreat of the individual, alienated from the social community; the domination or rejection of nature by spirit— these all have roots in the apocalyptic—Platonic religious heritage of classical Christianity. But the alienation of the masculine from the feminine is the primary sexual symbolism that sums up all these alienations. The psychic traits of intellectuality, transcendent spirit, and autonomous will that were identified with the male left the woman with the contrary traits of bodiliness, sensuality, and subjugation. Society, through the centuries, has in every way profoundly conditioned men and women to play out their lives and find their capacities within this basic antithesis.[8]

The insights gained from this perspective on the origins of both Judaism and Christianity remained primarily within the religious community during the earlier period of the movement. Many women influenced by this thinking, like Reuther, were active in issues of social justice and peace, and many churches housed women's consciousness-raising groups, domestic-violence shelters, day-care centers and a host of women-oriented services; but politics and religion made uneasy partners.

Moreover, the church often seemed to political women as more of an obstacle than an ally. This was especially the case as women faced increasing opposition around the issue of abortion and the ERA. Any concept of spirituality outside the confines of organized religion was especially suspect. This attitude toward religion and spirituality by the "political feminists" was captured in the mid-1970s by two women arguing for a greater relationship between them:

> Some . . . have seen spirituality as identified only with what patriarchy has said it to be—that is, a lot of male words, doctrines, laws, decrees and female suffering, poverty, chastity, and obedience. They have feared that women's traditional preoccupation with spiritual matters—if repeated in the women's movement—will divert us from political and economic struggles. Their political analysis has shown how religion has kept people from dealing with the social structures that oppress them. Many have decided that religion is but a reflection and expression of a particular culture, and therefore, religion as we know it, oppresses only because it reflects a patriarchal culture. Questions of spirituality are considered unresolvable until better social conditions are realized.[9]

While women argued to keep politics and religion separate, few envisioned a time when WITCH would mean anything more than a fun-loving, often wildly humorous group of women on the fringes who added lightness to the serious struggle.

Politics and Spirituality

The relationship between politics and spirituality in America is complex and often contradictory. We view ourselves as a nation founded with a "divine mission," pride ourselves in our separation of church and state, and like to think that we have established government free from religious prejudice. We worry about what happens when we bring the two together. During the 1984 presidential campaign, while both sexism and racism were evident, there was much public speculation about Geraldine Ferraro as a Catholic and of Jesse Jackson as a Baptist minister.

Many historians note the relationship between the Great Awakenings and subsequent political struggles. The social movements of this century have been fueled by religion and spiritual concerns. Martin Luther King, Jr. and Malcolm X, after all, were more than political leaders.

By the late 1970s and early 1980s, there was increasing evidence of a renewed concern for the connection between spirituality and politics. On a global scale we witnessed the Iranian Revolution and the revolutionary power of Islam, the victory of the Sandinistas and the impact of Liberation Theology throughout Central America, the emergence of Solidarity in Poland, the indictment of the spiritual emptiness of the bureaucratic state and the tremendous growth of the Religious Right in the United States. Whatever the strengths and weaknesses of these movements, they attest to the growing recognition of the spiritual emptiness of Western Culture and the technological society. Neither capitalism nor socialism as conceived and evolved in the modern era answer deeply felt spiritual needs.

For many women in this country, the questioning of Western culture and the re-discovery and re-creation of women's spirituality has begun to point a way to a very new kind of politics.

This new political and spiritual vision was articulated

early by Sally Gearhart. Consciously anti-capitalist and concerned about economic and social transformation, she concluded that there were four possible strategies for social change: violent revolutionary actions against the system; seizing power within the system; building alternative organizations and structures; or energy re-sourcement. By the mid-1970s she believed the first three strategies had "already lost."[10]

She argued for the creation of a very new politic that had to begin at a deeper level of "cosmic energy." She explained her "fourth strategy:"

> That new source is discovered only by moving inward to the self, and it is being experienced most widely these days by women who are finding our individual or intrapersonal energy flow. Once we are at home there—as more and more of us are becoming—then we can begin to develop authentic forms of interpersonal energy or that energy which flows between people. . . .

> What I am calling re-sourcement is the activity of women who are reaching out for new ways of understanding and viewing reality, i.e., *they are articulating a new epistimology:* astrology, the Tarot, numerology, the I Ching, the Kabala—all these and others reinterpreted and/or redeemed from their masculist emphases and filtered anew . . .[11]

This re-sourcement will lead to a new value system, a new ethic, a new sense of power free from domination and, ultimately, to a new society.

At the time Gearhart articulated this vision it was to a minority of women. But within a few years, that minority has grown.

The Spirit Healer

Signs of the new political/spiritual movement are everywhere. Demonstrations beginning with meditations, chants and songs have been joined by the call of women wailing ancient cries. Women meet around the country in small groups at the moment of the full moon to envision peace. Covens gather to celebrate the solstice. Political actions combine traditional pickets with groups of witches casting spells. Judges are not only watched, but groups meditate to direct their decisions. Conferences are called around the country bringing together nuns, lay women, women priests, preachers, witches, psychics, channelers, healers with herbs and touch and interested folk to discuss everything from political strategy to the healing power of crystals. By the mid-1980s, this activity reached the pages of *Ms. Magazine*. Long-standing political contributors like Deena Metzger and Karen Lindsey began to talk about these new political/spiritual forces.

The emerging spirituality is of course moving many women into contemplation and mysticism. For some it has become a justification for acceptance and inaction. But it is also encouraging public confrontation and political action. It undergirds the establishment of peace camps at Greenham Common and at Seneca Falls. It is the basis of much of the leadership women are providing to the anti-nuclear, disarmament and solidarity movements, and it is central to the growing emphasis on non-violent principles and practices which women are bringing to a host of national and community-based struggles.

This fusion of politics and spirituality is reflected in two distinct groupings. First are the traditional religious feminists, called reformists by Christ and Plaskow.[12] These women accept the basic validity of established religious experience but work to bring a feminist perspective to the interpretation of doctrine. They advocate a larger public role for women, the creation of women-centered religious rites, feminist liturgy and equal responsibility in administering all rites of the church or synagogue. Explaining the allegiance to existing institutions, despite its male perspective, Elisabeth Schussler Fiorenza says:

> It is, however, not so much theology but my own experience as a woman having grown up in the Catholic tradition that leads me to question that maleness is the essence of Christian faith and theology. Despite all masculine terminology of prayers, catechism, and liturgy, despite blatant patriarchal male spiritual guidance, my commitment to Christian faith and love first led me to question the feminine cultural role which parents, schools and church had taught me to accept and to internalize. My vision of Christian life-style brought me to reject the culturally imposed role of women and not vice versa.[13]

The second group, called the revolutionaries by Christ and Plaskow, are the witches and spiritual teachers. The most radical of the new feminists, they reject all established religion. Some are pagans, drawing upon early memory and re-membering of witchcraft practiced before the Christian era, others draw upon a sense of spirituality in nature and in practice such as meditation, laying on of hands, use of herbs and healing methods. They are also active in creating new political forms such as energy circles, covens and webs.

What do they believe?

Whatever the differences of doctrine or style, reformist or revolutionary, these women see themselves as representing a new understanding of the world which is essential if we are to avoid the destruction of ourselves and our planet and move to the 21st century with values that honor life. The core of these values reflects a coherent philosophical vision which is in stark contrast to that of the dominant culture.

Re-claiming and re-membering the past.

Much of the exploration of feminist spirituality, or of "womanspirit," begins with a reinterpretation of the origins of the modern world. Looking back to ancient cultures, women reexamine myths, archeological evidence, traditions and perspectives to argue that the beginnings of human development rested on matrilocal and matrifocal cultures. Women and their children were the basis of social group-ings and for centuries human beings lived peacefully, cooperatively, respecting and caring for one another and for the world. In the transition to agriculture women were brought under the control of men, who used power to dominate and control nature and everything in it. Conse-quently we all now have inherited a world view which separates us from nature, from one another and from our own past. This world view is at the root of the destruc-tiveness of modern society and must be overcome if we are to have any kind of a future at all.

The development of the view of a past based on prin-ciples and practices free from domination has produced a wealth of material from scholarly articles and books to adventure novels and movies. And precisely because it deals with a time that is unknowable by our current practices, it has provoked a great deal of argument. Much of the argu-ment against this view of the past, however, misses the point. Women do not intend simply to demonstrate that there was once a time when we had power. Rather, they argue that at this moment in history we need a new under-standing of our past in order to envision a new future. Only by enlarging our view of who we were, can we begin to imagine ourselves living very differently. Marilyn French, in *Beyond Power,* explains that we need to break out of the images and myths which govern our thinking or we will only be able to dig ourselves deeper into the present crisis. She writes:

> Humans have reached a stage from which it is almost impossible to imagine a future. This has not been true in the past. Those who anticipated the end of the world, a final day of judgment, also envisioned an afterlife in paradise, with their enemies properly installed in hell. The past few centuries have entertained dreams of progress, in which technology would free the human race from its burdens. If the future imagined by people of past ages was not the future that actually evolved, the two bore some resemblance to each other. But we cannot envision even a continuation of the present: we are utterly bankrupt of vision. And the barrenness of our imagination, our hope and faith, could result in the annihilation of our race.[14]

Reclaiming the past, then, becomes central to projecting the possibility of the future.

Experience as a way of knowing.

Of course, from the very beginning of the women's movement, day-to-day experience played a special role. The essence of consciousness-raising was the sharing of our personal lives. And it was the valuing of these experiences which advanced the idea of "the personal is political." The recognition of the power of reflecting, sharing and comparing our lives has led to a deeper understanding of how we construct knowledge and how we make judgments about ethics and action. The importance of this process in developing a new theology is discussed by Sheila Collins in her speech on "Theology in the Politics of Appalachian Women." She explains:

> So much of the old language has been corrupted beyond recognition that we must write our own dictionary from the words that express best our own experience and the experience of the as-yet-unarticulated lives of our sisters past and present. This does not mean that we throw out the Christian tradition. On the contrary, what we must do is learn to reappropriate that faith history in a new way. Some language will have to be discarded; other language turned inside out. But we cannot find the handles of reappropriation until we have gone through the process of collective, politicized storytelling and the collection of language for a new dictionary.
>
> . . . Through the telling and retelling of our stories, the inessentials are gradually sloughed off, until only the veins, the life-bearing vessels, remain. It is then that we begin to see the patterns of triumph, steadfastness, of salvation and liberation inherent in them. Just as the early Hebrews and early Christians looked back over their lives and discovered these patterns, so we discover what it was in women's experience that has kept women going through tragedy and devastation, through the daily rituals of feeding and caring. We discover the secret that keeps hope more alive in the oppressed who are conscious of the source of their oppression than in those who do the oppressing. Only then can we name that which has brought us through as the

God of *our* experiences—not the God of an alien and imposed culture. Only then can we distinguish with any clarity the true prophets from the false.[15]

Moving from the inside, out.

Women's experience provides the basis for the development of new connections among the personal, spiritual and political aspects of our lives. Change begins from the inside. The power and insight found in our inner dimensions enables us to change ourselves and the outer world in ways that honor and protect humanity. Margo Adair in her book *Working Inside Out* captures this dialectic in the introduction:

When you come to have a better understanding of consciousness, of the imagination, and creativity itself, and the relation they all have to the world around you then you won't feel so powerless—so buffeted about by all the turmoil. Instead you can tap the powers within you and fully employ your creativity to deal with the issues more effectively. When you are not at the will of all that's going on about you, you will be free to participate with clarity and vision—a very different feeling from that of being under pressure and constantly on the run just to keep up.[16]

The connectedness of struggles.

Spirituality is essentially about our feelings of connectedness to one another. For politically conscious women this means overcoming the fragmentation and isolation of not only our individual selves but our seemingly separate political struggles. Women have the obligation to move from their own oppression to work for the elimination of all relationships of control and domination. A recognition of the

fundamental relationship among what often appear to be
different forms of oppression is found throughout the writing
of most of the feminist spiritualists who are politically active. Sheila Collins writes:

> Racism, sexism, class exploitation, and ecological
> destruction are everywhere the same, although the
> particular forms in which oppression is manifested
> may at first glance look different. The democracy
> of the Athenian polis, to which the Western world
> has always looked as its ideal, was made possible
> only through the restricted domestic labors of the
> slaves and wives of the Athenian property owners.
> Western 'freedom' and affluence depend on the
> domestication of women and the exploitation of low-
> paid labor base made up of minorities and women
> as well as unlimited access to foreign sources of
> natural resources which are taken from the ground
> without regard for the rights of the Earth or the
> people who live on the land.[17]

The celebration of diversity.

The recognition of interconnectedness need not lead to
a blurring of distinctions or the denial of separate historical
experiences. Rather, differences need to be respected so we
can create a society in which we see diversity as an element
of strength. In her envisioning the future Margo Adair ex-
emplifies this notion:

> Imagine how it feels to always belong—belong in
> a diversified community, for it is the diversity in
> nature that gives the web of life strength and cohe-
> sion. Imagine a time where everyone welcomes
> diversity in people because they know that is what

gives community its richness, its strength, its cohesion. Imagine being able to relax into our connectedness—into a web of mutually supportive relations with each other and with nature.[18]

These beliefs provide a context for enriching and diverse spiritual practices: energy circles, meditation, the creation of women's liturgy and ritual, the development of covens and the casting of circles and spells. And they have profound implications for the ethics of a new society and culture. Nonhierarchal, cooperative, supportive, peaceful, balanced relations with one another and with nature are all central to this vision.

Where are we going?

Thus, the emerging feminist-spiritual vision holds the promise of not only healing individual women and men, but of providing the spiritual and political energy to heal our world.

This radical potential, however, is slow in moving from theory to practice. While the feminist spiritualists acknowledge the connectedness to all struggles and the need to work on outer transformation as well as inner growth, there are only small signs that some few among them are actually creating forms where this is possible. Most of this theory seems a long way from the life of the underclass. What does it mean to the women working and waiting on lines, feeding their families and worrying about day-to-day issues?

The division between the theoretical advances and the practical work of women today can be seen in the movements in which they are giving leadership. Anti-nuclear, disarmament, solidarity struggles, and ecology movements—these are still made up of predominantly white, middle-class members and have not as yet been able conceptually or practically to make connections to community based struggles, where women are often moving.

The division between politics and spirituality and the separation between theory and practice which are so striking among those who identify as feminist, does not exist for many women at the bottom of our society who are working to rebuild community life. For the Native American women leading the struggle at Big Mountain, for Appalachian women fighting strip mining and land development, for the mothers of children killed in Detroit organizing to stop the shootings, life itself is more integrated. Many of these women, who would never consider themselves feminists, are giving leadership to struggles because their lives and the lives of their children depend on fundamental change.

These struggles reflect the experience of people who have traditionally resisted the kind of divisions in Western culture which have created a politics free from ethics and values. It is these efforts of women facing basic issues about the existence of their children and community which hold the most potential for change in the country today. The challenge for feminists is how to support and contribute to these ongoing struggles.

As powerful as the theoretical contributions may be, then, they often reflect the particular "blind spot" endemic to a society infused with race and class divisions. These works lack acknowledgment of the role spirituality has traditionally played in the struggles and daily lives of African Americans, Native Americans, people of color and ethnic communities. By drawing so heavily on the experience of women most active in the "movement," or the ancient past, these insights lack the strength that comes from those who have continually resisted in their ordinary lives the rational, objective view of reality forged by the dominant society. The old woman down the street who offers catnip tea to sooth teething children, the mother who uses potatoes to cure warts or the woman who asks for healing prayers all experience a form of spiritual connectedness that is too often outside the view of this new political and spiritual vision. The vision itself, then, suffers from the lack of connection to living communities.

One of the central challenges to the emerging image of woman as Spirit Healer is the recognition that while our vision must grow out of our experience as women, the experience of all women is not the same. In our country, shaped and developed by racism and capitalism, those groups who have traditionally been kept out of the "mainstream" have maintained a sense of humanity less eroded by industrial culture. There are still those among us who remember a different time, who have a sense of tradition, of wholeness, of ritual and integrity, who can offer their voices to a vision of a new future. For these voices to be heard will require a new openness and humility among feminists.

Before us are two very different futures. The Spirit Healer can be perverted to protect power and privilege, and serve as a justification for passivity, suffering and oppression. Or it can help lead us toward a radically different future based on cooperation and a sense of the sacred which is life affirming and sustaining. Critical to the direction we take is our capacity to look deeply into the history of our country as well as into our selves. Our vision needs to be rooted in the reality of those among us who have consistently resisted the dehumanization of industrial America and who are struggling today to preserve a sense of dignity for themselves and for their children. Without these roots, the new Spirit Healer will be little more than an intellectual fad.

184

For a little while, we have time to struggle with this choice.

S.H.
Detroit, Michigan
June, 1987

NOTES

1. Charlene Spretnak, "The Christian Right's 'Holy War' Against Feminism," in Charlene Spretnak, ed., *The Politics of Women's Spirituality*, (New York: Anchor Books, 1982), pp. 470–496.

2. James D. Squires, ed., *The American Millstone: An Examination of the Nation's Permanent Underclass*, (Chicago: Contemporary Books, Inc., 1986), pp. 4–5.

3. Ibid, p. 12.

4. Carolyn J. Jacobsen, "Meeting the Challenge of Job and Family," *Women at Work*, AFL-CIO American Federationist, April 5, 1986, pp. 1–2.

5. Jeffrey Weeks, *Sexuality and its Discontents: Meanings, Myths & Modern Sexualities*, (London: Routledge & Kegan Paul, 1985).

6. Sally Gearhart, "Womanpower: Energy Re-Sourcement," in *The Politics of Women's Spirituality*, p. 205.

7. Lillian S. Robinson, *Sex, Class and Culture*, (New York: Menthuen, 1978), pp. 47–49.

8. Rosemary Radford Ruether, "Motherearth and the Megamachine: A Theology of Liberation in a Feminine, Somatic and Ecological Perspective," Carol Christ and Judith Plaskow, eds., *Womanspirit Rising*, (New York: Harper and Row Publishers, 1979), p. 44.

9. Judy Davis and Juanita Weaver, "Dimensions of Spirituality," in *The Politics of Women's Spirituality*, p. 371.

10. Gearhart, p. 195.

11. Ibid, pp. 195–196.

12. Christ and Plaskow, pp. 10–11.

13. Elisabeth Schussler Fiorenza, "Feminist Spirituality, Christian Identity, and Catholic Vision," in *Womanspirit Rising*, p. 137

14. Marilyn French, *Beyond Power*, (New York: Ballantine Books, 1985), p. 15.

15. Sheila Collins, "Theology in the Politics of Appalachian Women ," in *Womanspirit Rising*, pp. 154–155.

16. Margo Adair, *Working Inside Out: Tools for Change,* Berkley: Wingbow Press, 1984), p. 1.

17. Sheila Collins, "The Personal is Political," in *The Politics of Women's Spirituality,* p. 363.

18. Adair, p. 284.

BIBLIOGRAPHY

Andrews, James R. "History and Theory in the Study of the Rhetoric of Social Movements." *Central States Speech Journal* 31: 274–282.

Arendt, Hannah. *On Revolution.* New York: Penguin Books, 1977.

Atkinson, Ti-Grace. "Theories of Radical Feminism." *Notes from the Second Year: Women's Liberation.* Edited by Shulamith Firestone. New York: Signet, 1970.

Beard, Mary R. *Women as Force in History.* New York: Collier Books, 1972.

Bitzer, Lloyd F. "The Rhetorical Situation." *Philosophy and Rhetoric.* Winter. 1968.

_____. "Rhetoric and Public Knowledge." *Rhetoric, Philosophy and Literature: An Exploration.* Edited by Don Burks. West Lafayette, Indiana: Purdue University Press, 1978.

Bormann, Ernest G. "Fantasy and Rhetorical Vision: The Rhetorical Criticism of Social Reality." *Quarterly Journal of Speech* 58:

Bosmajian, Haig A., ed. *Dissent: Symbolic Behavior and Rhetorical Strategies.* Boston: Allyn and Bacon, 1972.

Boulding, Elise. *The Underside of History: A View of Women Through Time.* Boulder, Colorado: Westview Press, 1976.

Bowers, John W. and Ochs, Donovan J. *The Rhetoric of Agitation and Control.* Reading, Mass.: Addison-Wesley, 1971.

Brownmiller, Susan. *Against Our Will: Men, Women and Rape.* New York: Simon and Schuster, 1975.

Burke, Kenneth. *Attitudes Toward History.* Boston: Beacon Press, 1955.

Cathcart, Robert. "Defining Social Movements by their Rhetorical Form." *Central States Speech Journal* 31: 267–272.

_____. "Movements: Confrontation as Rhetorical Form." *Southern States Speech Communication Journal* 43:

_____. "New Approaches to the Study of Movements: Defining Movements Rhetorically." *Western Speech* 36:

Campbell, Karlyn Kohrs. *Critique of Contemporary Rhetoric.* Belmont, California: Wadsworth Publishing Co., 1972.

_____. "The Rhetoric of Women's Liberation: An Oxymoron." *Quarterly Journal of Speech* 59: 1973.

_____. "Stanton's 'The Solitude of Self': A Rationale for Feminism. *Quarterly Journal of Speech* 66: 304–312.

Campbell, Paul Newel. "Metaphor and Linguistic Theory." *Quarterly Journal of Speech* 61: 325–333.

Carroll, Bernice A. "Political Science, Part I: American Politics and Political Behavior." *Signs: Journal of Women in Culture* 5: 289–306.

Cheseboro, James W. "Rhetorical Strategies of the Radical Revolutionary." *Today's Speech* 20: 45–52.

Conrad, Charles. "The Transformation of the 'Old Feminist' Movement." *Quarterly Journal of Speech* 67: 1981.

Cooke, Joanne; Bunch-Weeks, Charlotte; and Morgan, Robin, eds. *The New Woman.* Greenwich, Conn: Fawcett, 1969.

Davis, Angela. "Joanne Little: The Dialectics of Rape." *Ms.* (June, 1975): 77–83.

Deckard, Barbara. *The Women's Movement.* New York: Harper and Row, 1975.

Decter, Midge. *The New Chastity and other Arguments against Women's Liberation.* New York: Berkeley Medallion Books, 1972.

Dinnerstein, Dorothy. *The Mermaid and the Minatour.* New York: Harper Colophon, 1976.

Elshtain, Jean Bethke. "The Anti-Feminist Backlash," *Commonweal* 8: (March 1974): 16–19.

190

_____. *Public Man, Private Woman.* Princeton, New Jersey: Princeton University Press, 1981.

_____. *Review of Against our Will.* Telos 30: 327–342.

Evans, Sara. *Personal Politics: The Origins of the Women's Movement in the Civil Rights Movement.* New York: Vintage Books, 1980.

Freeman, Jo. *The Politics of Women's Liberation.* New York: David McKay, 1975.

Friedan, Betty. *It Changed My Life.* New York: Dell, 1977.

Griffin, Leland. "On Studying Movements." *Central States Speech Journal* 31: 225–232.

Golden, James L.; Berquist, Goddwin F. and Coleman, William F. *The Rhetoric of Western Thought.* Dubuque, Iowa: Kendall/Hunt Publishing Co., 1976.

Gornick, Vivian and Moran, Barbara K., eds. *Women in Sexist Society: Studies in Power and Powerlessness.* New York: Signet, 1971.

Grossberg, Lawrence. "Marxist Dialectics and Rhetorial Criticism. *Quarterly Journal of Speech* 65: 235–249.

Hahn, Dan F. and Gonchar, Ruth M. "Studying Social Movements: A Rhetorical Methodology." *Speech Teacher* 20: 42–58.

Halloran, Michael. "Public vs. Private: Richard Sennett on Public Life and Authority." *Quarterly Journal of Speech* 67: 322–323.

Henley, Nancy. *Body Politics: Power, Sex and Nonverbal Communication.* Englewood Cliffs, New Jersey: Prentice-Hall, 1977.

Hole, Judith and Levin, Ellen. *Rebirth of Feminism.* New York: Quadrangle Books, Inc., 1971.

Hope, Diane Schaich. "Redefinition of Self: A Comparison of the Rhetoric of the Woman's Liberation and Black Liberation Movements." *Today's Speech.* Winter, 1975: 20-26.

Janeway, Elizabeth. *Man's World, Woman's Place.* New York: Delta Books, 1971.

_____. "Who is Sylvia? On the Loss of Sexual Paradigms," *Signs: Journal of Women in Culture and Society* 5: 573-589.

Keck, Donna and Pappas, Dee Ann, eds. *Women: A Journal of Liberation.* Baltimore, Maryland, 1969.

Koedt, Anne; Levine, Ellen and Rapone, Anita. *Radical Feminism.* New York: Quadrangle Books, Inc., 1973.

Lakoff, George and Johnson, Mark. *Metaphors We Live By.* Chicago: University of Chicago Press, 1980.

Landes, Joan. "The Theory Behind Women's Liberation: Problems and Prospects." Ph.D. dissertation, New York University, 1975.

McGee, Michael. "The Ideograph: A Link Between Rhetoric and Ideology." *Quarterly Journal of Speech* 66: 1-16.

_____. "Social Movements: Phenomenon or Meaning?" *Central States Speech Journal* 31: 233-244.

Millet, Kate. *Sexual Politics.* Garden City, New Jersey: Doubleday, 1970.

Mitchell, Juliet. *Psychoanalysis and Feminism.* New York: Pantheon, 1971.

_____. *Woman's Estate.* New York: Vintage Books, 1973.

Okin, Susan Moller. *Women in Western Political Thought.* Princeton, New Jersey: Princeton University Press, 1979.

Osborn, Michael and Ehninger, Douglas. "The Metaphor in Public Address." *Speech Monographs* 29:

Piercy, Marge. *To Be of Use.* Garden City: Doubleday, 1969.

_____. *Woman on the Edge of Time.* New York: Fawcett, 1978.

Rosen-Wasser, Marie J. "Rhetoric and the Progress of the Women's Liberation Movement." *Today's Speech* 20: 45–56.

Rubin, Lillian. *Worlds of Pain: Life in the Working-Class Family.* New York: Basic Books, 1976.

Ruether, Rosemary Radford. "The Cult to True Womanhood." *Commonweal* (November, 1973): 127–132.

Rowbotham, Sheila. *Woman's Consciousness, Man's World.* Baltimore: Penguin Books, 1973.

_____. *Women, Resistance and Revolution.* New York: Vintage Books, 1972.

Saffioti, Heleieth. *Women in Class Society*. New York: Monthly Review Press, 1978.

Sapir, J. David and Crocker, J. Christopher. *The Social Use of Metaphor: Essays on the Anthropology of Rhetoric*. Philadelphia: University of Pennsylvania Press, 1977.

Schlafly, Phyllis. *The Power of the Positive Woman*. New York: Jove, 1977.

Sherman, Julia A. and Beck, Evelyn Torton, eds., *The Prism of Sex: Essays in the Sociology of Knowledge*. Madison: University of Wisconsin Press, 1979.

Shulman, Alix Kates. "Sex and Power: Sexual Basis of Radical Feminism." *Signs: Journal of Women in Culture and Society* 5: 590-604.

Simons, Herbert. "Requirements, Problems and Strategies: A Theory of Persuasion for Social Movements. *Quarterly Journal of Speech* 61: 1-19.

_____. "Simons on Bormann and Osborn." *Quarterly Journal of Speech* 66: 206-208.

_____. "Terms, Definitions and Theoretical Distinctiveness: Comments on Papers by McGee and Zarefsky." *Central States Speech Journal* 32: 306-315.

Sobel, Maxine. "Rage in Rochester: What Women Should Know." *New Times*. January, 1975: 7.

Solomon, Martha. "The 'Positive Woman's' Journey: A Mythic Analysis of the Rhetoric of Stop ERA." *Quarterly Journal of Speech* : 262-74.

Steinem, Gloria. "But What do We do with Our Rage?" *Ms.* (May 1975): 51–53.

Sykes, A.M.J. "Myth in Communication." *The Journal of Communication,* (March, 1980): 17–31.

Vatz, Richard. "The Myth of the Rhetorical Situation." *Philosophy and Rhetoric* 6: 154–161.

Warrior, Betsy. "Man as an Obsolete Life Form." *No More Fun and Games: A Journal of Female Liberation* 2: 77–78.

Wilkinson, Charles A. "A Rhetorical Definition of Movements." *Central States Speech Journal* 27: 92–98.

Zarefsky, David. "President Johnson's War on Povety: The Rhetoric of Three 'Establishment' Movements." *Communication Monographs* 44: 352–373.

_____. "A Skeptical View of Movement Studies." *Central States Speech Journal* 31: 245–254.